Eyewitness
CHINA

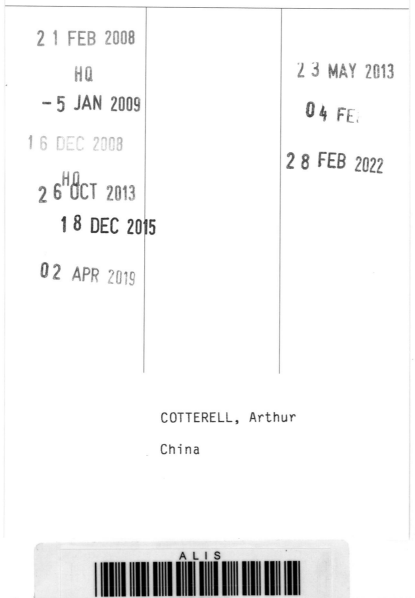

Harness ornaments, 7th–6th century B.C.

Sword and sheath, decorated with brass and tortoiseshell

Stucco head of a Bodhisattva, 8th–9th century

Sihu, or spike fiddle, and bow, 19th century

Carved lacquer boxes

Jade ear scoop and various bronze tweezers

Modern calligraphy brushes

Eyewitness
CHINA

Written by
ARTHUR COTTERELL

Photographed by
ALAN HILLS & GEOFF BRIGHTLING

...tery tomb
...res, 7th–8th
...tury

DK

Ivory necklace
for a civil servant,
early 20th century

DK

LONDON, NEW YORK, MELBOURNE,
MUNICH, and DELHI

Project editor Bridget Hopkinson
Art editor Jill Plank
Designer Ivan Finnegan
Managing editor Simon Adams
Managing art editor Julia Harris
Researcher Céline Carez
Production Catherine Semark
Picture research Lorna Ainger

PAPERBACK EDITION
Editors Barbara Berger, Laura Buller, Sue Nicholson
Editorial assistant John Searcy
Publishing director Beth Sutinis
Senior designer Tai Blanche
Designers Jessica Lasher, Diana Catherines, Rebecca Wright
Photo research Chrissy McIntyre
Art director Dirk Kaufman
DTP designers Milos Orlovic, Andy Hilliard
Production Ivor Parker, Angela Graef

This Eyewitness ® Book has been conceived by
Dorling Kindersley Limited and Editions Gallimard.

Hardback edition first published in Great Britain in 1994
This edition first published in Great Britain in 2006 by
Dorling Kindersley Limited,
80 Strand, London WC2R 0RL

2 4 6 8 10 9 7 5 3 1

A CIP catalogue record for this book is available from the British Library.

ISBN-10 1 4053 1494 X
ISBN-13 978 1 4053 1494 7

Typesetting by Litho Link Ltd, Welshpool, Powys
Colour reproduction by Colourscan, Singapore
Printed in China by Toppan Printing Co., (Shenzhen) Ltd.

Discover more at
www.dk.com

Fish-shaped
cloisonné
vase, 18th
century

Decorated model
sampan

Kitchen kni
and cas
19th centu

Ceremonial
Buddhist conch,
8th century

Contents

Inlaid bronze
chariot decoration,
4th century B.C.

The world's oldest empire

CHINA IS THE WORLD'S OLDEST continuous civilization. From 221 B.C. to A.D. 1912, it was united under a single great empire. Ancient China remained untouched by outside influences because it was a world apart. Vast deserts and mountain ranges cut off China from other cultures in India, West Asia, and Europe, and many hundreds of years passed before the Chinese realized in 126 B.C. that other civilizations existed. China's social structure played a key role in maintaining its national stability. The civil service established by the first Han emperor helped successive dynasties govern the huge population wisely and effectively. Chinese philosophers also made a significant contribution to social harmony. Great thinkers such as Confucius encouraged people to lead an ordered, family-orientated way of life.

CHINA UNITED
China was first united as a single state in 221 B.C. by the First Emperor. This map shows the boundaries of his empire. The Great Wall, seen at the top of the map, was built in about 214 B.C. and linked a series of older walls.

Qin empire

Bronze ritual water vessel, Zhou dynasty

Bronze ritual wine vessel, Shang dynasty

Bronze spearheads, Warring States period

Terracotta soldier, Qin dynasty

SHANG
China's first great dynasty was the Shang. This Bronze Age civilization is renowned for its skilful metalwork and for the emergence of the first Chinese writing. The Shang kings and their nobles ruled the mainly rural population from walled towns and cities. Horse-drawn chariots were the chief means of transport.

c. 1650–1027 B.C.

ZHOU
Confucius looked back on the early years of the Zhou dynasty as a golden age. The Zhou kings maintained the Shang practice of ancestor worship, and society was organized on a feudal system: great lords ruled the peasant farmers from large estates.

1027–256 B.C.

WARRING STATES PERIOD
As the Zhou declined, great lords fought each other for supremacy in what became known as the Warring States period. Vast armies clashed in large-scale battles and hundreds of thousands of men were killed. Confucius and other philosophers taught more peaceful ways of being, but their ideas were not adopted until later years.

481–221 B.C.

QIN
In 221 B.C. the First Emperor united China under the Qin dynasty. He built the Great Wall to protect his empire from the northern nomads and standardized Chinese script, coins, weights, and measures. The First Emperor united China so firmly that afterwards the Chinese people regarded imperial rule as the only form of government.

221–207 B.C.

Carved stone Buddha,
Tang dynasty

onze mirror,
an dynasty

Ceramic water vessel,
Period of disunity

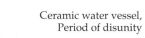

Engraved silver dish,
Tang dynasty

AN
e Han emperors consolidated the
perial system by establishing a
tional civil service that was to run
ina for the next 2,000 years.
ucated officials studied the
chings of Confucius and were
ected by a rigorous examination
stem. State factories manufactured
kinds of goods, from iron
oughshares to silk cloth.

PERIOD OF DISUNITY
In the Period of disunity, China
was divided into separate states,
although it was briefly united
under the Western Jin dynasty
(265–316). Foreign peoples
overran northern China, and in
the south, various dynasties
struggled for power. The gentle
ideas of Buddhism first became
popular in these years of unrest.

SUI
The Sui
dynasty reunified northern and
southern China. In their brief reign,
the Sui emperors rebuilt the Great
Wall and dug the Grand Canal.
This great waterway linked the
Yangzi and Yellow rivers, which
improved communications and
enabled grain and soldiers to be
transported around the empire.

TANG
Under the Tang emperors, the
Chinese empire expanded to
become a great world power. This
was a time of prosperity and
cultural renaissance in which both
art and trade flourished. The civil
service was reformed so that
officials were recruited by merit
rather than birth, and poetry was
added to the examination syllabus.

 B.C.–A.D. 220   221–589   589–618   618–906

Continued on next page

The empire continues

Although the Chinese empire experienced periods of unrest and disunity, and even conquests by foreign peoples, it existed as a strong state until modern times. China's borders ebbed and flowed with its changing dynasties, and the position of the imperial capital shifted several times, but the centralized government set up by the First Emperor survived for over 2,000 years. There were many great innovations and technological advances throughout the empire's long history. The inventions of gunpowder, paper, printing, and industrial machinery all had an effect on Chinese culture. Nevertheless, the customs and traditions of the Chinese people, particularly those of the rural population, stayed remarkably constant.

Kubilai Khan, the great Mongol ruler

Blue dish with a dragon motif, Song dynasty

Bronze flower vase, Song or Yuan dynasty

Blue and yellow glazed dish, Ming dynasty

Greenware dish, Yuan dynasty

FIVE DYNASTIES
In the Five Dynasties period, China was again briefly divided into north and south. A part of northern China fell under foreign rule, while the south was divided into numerous small states, many more than the name Five Dynasties implies. Southern China continued to prosper both culturally and economically.

907–960

SONG
China was united once more under the Song dynasty and reached its greatest heights of civilization. Advances in science and technology produced a minor industrial revolution, and the world's first mechanized industry was developed. Commodities such as iron and salt were produced on an industrial scale and were transported to distant parts of the empire on improved road and canal networks. The Song emperors were great patrons of the arts, and poetry, painting, and calligraphy reached new levels of perfection.

960–1279

YUAN
In the 13th century, China was conquered by the Mongols who established their own dynasty, the Yuan. Throughout Mongol rule, Chinese scholars were banned from the civil service and many of them retired to write literature. Because the Mongols controlled the entire length of the Silk Road, international trade thrived. Many merchants became rich by exporting Chinese luxury goods. Marco Polo, and later other Europeans, visited China and reported on the marvels of its civilization.

1279–1368

Cloisonné ewer,
Ming dynasty

Delicately painted
porcelain dish,
Qing dynasty

CHINA TODAY
The map below shows the present-day boundaries of China. It has remained a strong world power.

Russia

Mongolia

Great Wall

Beijing

Korea

Yellow River

Kaifeng

Xi'an

Luoyang

Nanjing

Shanghai

China

Hangzhou

Nepal

Bhutan

Bangladesh

India

Yangzi River

Burma

Taiwan

Hong Kong

Thailand

Laos

Vietnam

[MIN]G
r less than a hundred years, the Chinese drove the ngols out of China and replaced them with the last nese dynasty, the Ming. The Ming emperors set up w capital in Beijing, strengthened the Great Wall, improved the Grand Canal. They also attempted e-establish Chinese prestige by sending Admiral ng He on seven great maritime expeditions to visit ign rulers. Chinese culture flourished once again, the Ming dynasty became famous for its exquisite and crafts.

QING
The Chinese empire eventually collapsed under a foreign dynasty, the Manchu, or Qing dynasty. The Qing emperors lived in fear of a Chinese revolt and clung to outdated traditions. For the first time, Chinese technology fell behind other countries. Foreign powers began to demand trade concessions and, after a series of wars, China was forced to yield both concessions and territory. In 1911 the Chinese overthrew the weakened Qing government and formed a republic. The Last Emperor stepped down in 1912.

AFTER THE EMPIRE
The Chinese republic established in 1912 lasted for only 37 years. It was destroyed by war with Japan and, after the Second World War, civil conflict. In the civil war between 1946 to 1949, Communist forces were victorious. The Chinese Communist Party set up the present-day People's Republic of China in 1949.

–1644

1644–1912

1912– present

Jade *cong*,
c. 2500 B.C.

Jade axehead,
eastern China
c. 4500–2500 B.C.

PRE-SHANG JADES
These ancient jades were probably
used in Neolithic rituals concerned
with death. The *cong* may have
represented the earthly powers.

The beginning of China

THE FIRSTS CHINESE DYNASTY to leave a historical record was the Shang. The Shang kings ruled the greater part of northern China from about 1650 to 1027 B.C. The Shang ruler was a kind of priest-king, known as the Son of Heaven. He was believed to be vested with all earthly powers and was expected to maintain good relation between earth and the heavenly realm. The spirits of the royal ancestors were consulted on every important decision. The king alone possessed the authority to ask for their blessings, and he held the power to ward off ancestral ill-will. Although the Shang rulers had many slaves, they relied upon the labour of their mainly rural population. The peasant farmers cultivated the land, took part in royal hunts, and served as foot soldiers in the army.

*A bronze blade
easy to cast
deadly on
battlef*

*The halberd was moun
horizontally and was
swung like a scythe*

LETHAL WEAPON
The halberd, a dagger-shaped blade, was a favourite weapon of war from Shang times onwards. It was carried by foot soldiers and also swung at the enemy from speeding chariots. However, most fighting took place on foot with spears and small knives.

*Light brown jade
with beautiful
grey streaks*

*Ea
l*

Taotie
*mon
face, a pop
Shang m*

Eye

Mouth

RITUAL CAULDRO
The Shang made offerings of food a drink to the spirits their ancestors in special religious ceremonies. Food prepared for the d as if it were a banq for the living. It wa served to the ancestors in highly decorated bronze vessels like this *din*

HEAVENLY SPHERE
This jade disc is called a *bi*. Large numbers of *bi* have been found in Neolithic burial sites in China, along with *cong* and axeheads. These precious objects were laid along the limbs of the dead; the circular *bi* seems to have represented Heaven. Similar discs were used in the Shang dynasty. In Shang belief, the high god of Heaven, Shang Di, blessed the ruler with good harvests, victories on the battlefield, and strong sons. All important questions were referred to the spirits of the royal ancestors in the heavenly realm before decisions were made.

Bronze socketed
axeheads,
12th–11th
century B.C.

*Taotie
motif*

AXE BLADES
These axes may
have been carried
by royal soldiers.
The Shang army
comprised a body
of regulars who
were reinforced by
peasant farmers in
times of crisis. The
king summoned the
nobles to war, and
they called up the
peasant farmers.

*The wine container
was the most
common kind of
ritual vessel*

*Chinese writing
evolved from this
kind of Shang
script*

Crack

WINE CUP
The Shang used about 20 different
kinds of sacrificial vessel for ancestor
worship. One of the most striking
was a cup known as a *jue*. Wine
was poured from its beak-like
spout to honour the
ancestral spirits.

Spout

*Delicate
edging*

*Taotie
motif*

BRONZE STAFF-HEAD
The skill of the Shang in
casting decorative bronzes
was unmatched, as this
beautiful bronze staff-head
shows. However, it is doubtful
whether bronze tools were
available to farmers, who still
used stone implements.
Metallurgy was a royal
industry and bronze foundries
were situated close to towns,
where they were supervised
by the king's officials.

ORACLE BONE
The Shang kings used oracle
bones to consult the ancestral
spirits on important matters.
An ox bone or tortoiseshell
was scorched until it cracked.
The cracks were then read to
discover the answer to a
question put to the ancestors.
Often, the questions and
answers were inscribed on
the oracle bone.

CEREMONIAL BEAKER
This tall, slender beaker is a *gu*.
It was used for drinking wine
and, like the *jue*, for pouring
wine in honour of the
ancestors. Nearly all of the
bronze vessels used for
ancestor worship were based
on everyday pottery utensils.
The king and nobles owned
the largest, most ornate ritual
vessels, while poorer families
used pottery copies.

The teachings of Confucius

Confucius, the "uncrowned emperor" of China; his ideas shaped Chinese thought for several millennia

CONFUCIUS BELIEVED that the early years of the Zhou dynasty (1027–256 B.C.) were golden years of social harmony. In his own lifetime (551–479 B.C.) Confucius saw only growing disorder. The king's authority was greatly reduced as ambitious lords fought each other for power. This increasing turmoil led Confucius to develop a new moral outlook. It was based on kindness, respect, and the strength of the family. He said that a good ruler should set an example by dealing fairly with his subjects, using force only as a last resort. In return, subjects had a duty to respect and obey their ruler. Confucius believed that family relationships should be governed by the same principles of mutual respect, since strong families formed the basis of a stable society. He summed up his philosophy when he said: "Let the prince be a prince, the minister a minister, the father a father, and the son a son." Confucius encouraged ancestor worship because it strengthened family loyalties. As a result, the Chinese came to see themselves as part of a great family that encompassed not only the living, but also the dead and the unborn.

Bell was hung on a loop to allow it to vibrate clearly

Large bronze be 6th–5th century B

ZHOU CHIMES
The Chinese believed the music of bells calmed the mind and aided thought. On hearing a piece of ritual music, Confucius was inspired to spurn worldly comforts and live on water and rice for three months.

Bell had no clapper inside; it was struck on the outside like a gong

Ear

Spiky horn

Horse-like face

RITES OF PASSAGE
Confucius had good reason to regard the first Zhou kings as ideal rulers. After the death of the last Shang king in 1027 B.C., the victorious Zhou leader, Wu, showed proper respect for the fallen royal house by arranging for the continuation of ancestral rites. This sacrificial vessel was used for ancestor worship in the early Zhou period.

Side view

Zhou bronze ritual vessel, or *gui*, 11th-century B.C.

To establish the date, the inscription begins by noting that the Zhou king had been attacking the remnants of the defeated Shang kingdom

Handle in the form of a mythical beast

A MESSAGE TO THE ANCESTORS
An inscription inside this sacrificial vessel records the grant of territory or office to a friend of the Duke of Kang, a brother of the Zhou king Wu. Placing inscriptions inside ritual vessels was common practice among Zhou nobles. They recorded honours and gifts bestowed upon them by the king. The Zhou nobles believed that their ancestors would learn of their achievements when the vessels were used in the rituals of ancestor worship.

The script used to inscribe ritual vessels evolved into one of the most renowned forms of early Chinese writing

Overhead view

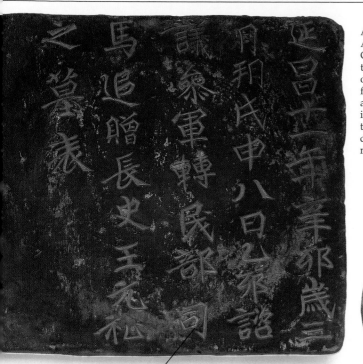

A DISTINGUISHED ANCESTOR
Ancestor worship became an important Chinese tradition. Offerings were made to the ancestors at the festival of Qingming once a year. This clay epitaph tablet stood in front of the tomb of Wang Yuanzhi, a senior administrator in the civil service who died in A.D. 571. The tablet served as a reminder to Wang Yuanzhi's descendants of his distinguished career. They would have made offerings before it during Qingming.

FEARSOME GUARDIAN
Relatives conducted the annual rite of ancestor worship at the entrance to their ancestor's tomb. From the Han dynasty onwards, every wealthy person had a brick-built underground tomb decorated with pressed bricks or wall paintings. The tomb was covered by a mound and enclosed within a sacred area. Ancestor worshippers approached along a spirit path lined with carvings of animals and sometimes people.

Tomb guardian, or *qitou*, Tang dynasty

Characters incised in clay, then painted red

Painted mane

FABULOUS TOMB ANIMAL
Confucius was against slavery and human or animal sacrifices. Under his influence, it became common practice to place pottery figures inside tombs instead of living slaves and animals. This strange pottery animal was found in a tomb that dates from the 4th century A.D. It was probably intended to ward off evil influences.

Snaky tail

Cow-like body

Cloven hoof

The art of war

Guan Di the Confucian god of war, worshipped for his ability to prevent conflicts as well as for his heroic character

THREE CENTURIES OF BRUTAL WARFARE marked the decline of the Zhou dynasty. The Zhou became unable to control disputes among the great lords, and by 481 B.C. China had separated into seven warring states. Battles became large-scale contests with armoured infantry, crossbowmen, cavalry, and chariots. Thousands of men were killed or wounded. At the battle of Chang Ping in 260 B.C., over half a million men are known to have fallen. During this period Sun Zi wrote *The Art of War*, the world's oldest military handbook, which gave advice to nobles on the practice of warfare. Eventually the north-western state of Qin was victorious and, in 221 B.C., united the feuding lords under a single empire. In later years, the military declined in status. The civil service grew in importance and the gentler ideas of Confucianism prevailed.

Harness ornament fitted along the horse's cheek

Taotie, or monster face, decoration

Scabbard and dagger, 7th–6th century B.C.

Gold harness ornaments with *taotie* design, 7th–6th century B.C.

HARNESS ORNAMENTS
These ornate harness attachments decorated the the harnesses of cavalry horses. Although battles largely became contests between massed ranks of foot soldiers, or infantry, the cavalry were still used for lightning attacks and for the defence of the infantry's flanks.

SWORD PLAY
Military success was displayed in fine weapons, such as this bronze dagger and sword. However, bronze weapons never achieved the same status that the medieval sword did in Europe. In imperial China, peaceful Confucian virtues were revered over the art of warfare.

SHOW OF STRENGTH
This horse frontlet fitted along the nose of a chariot horse. Both harnesses and chariots were decorated to heighten the magnificent spectacle of the chariots in battle. These splendid vehicles were important status symbols. They were buried with their owners, along with the horses and charioteers.

Bronze horse bit, Han dynasty

Bronze nose-guard for a chariot horse

Bronze axle cap protected the axle of a chariot wheel

HORSEPOWER
This delicate bit was probably worn by a cavalry horse in the Han dynasty. Chinese cavalrymen rode the small Mongolian pony until the Han emperor Wu Di obtained bigger horses from Central Asia in 101 B.C. This greatly improved the strength of the cavalry. The larger horses were faster and could carry more heavily armoured men.

ANCIENT AXLE CAPS
Chariots were made of wood and were pulled by two or four horses. Their wheels raised them high above the ground. They usually carried three men: a charioteer, an archer, and a halberdier. The management of a chariot was considered an essential skill for a noble.

Sword, 4th century B.C.

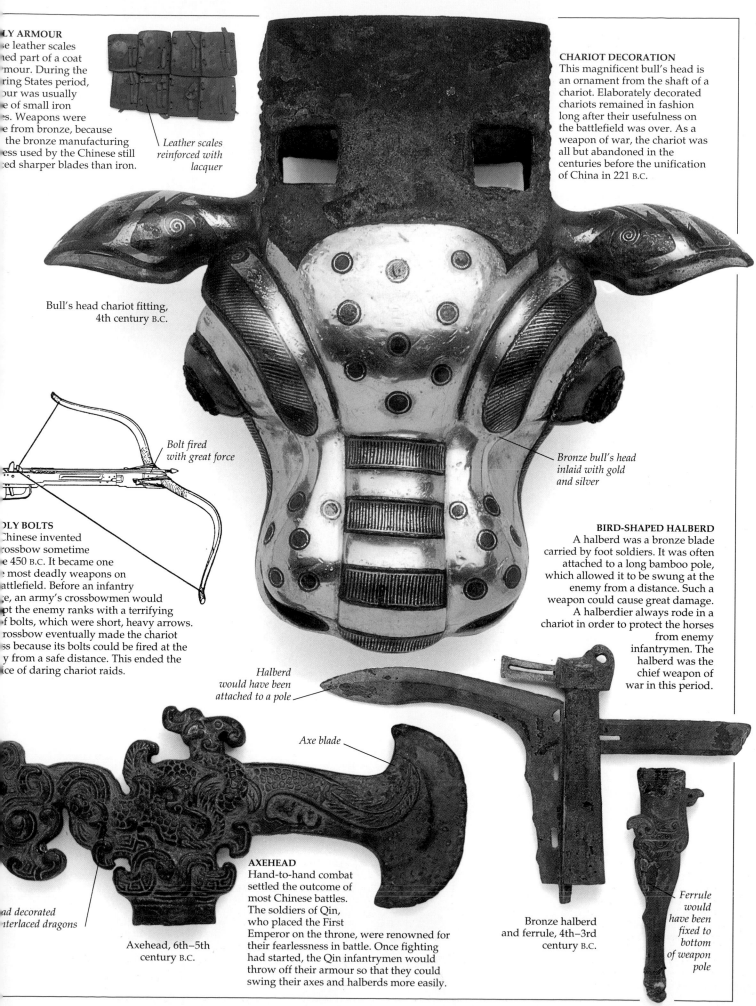

...e leather scales
...ed part of a coat
...rmour. During the
...ring States period,
...ur was usually
...e of small iron
...s. Weapons were
...e from bronze, because
...the bronze manufacturing
...ss used by the Chinese still
...ed sharper blades than iron.

*Leather scales
reinforced with
lacquer*

*Bull's head chariot fitting,
4th century* B.C.

*Bolt fired
with great force*

...LY BOLTS
...Chinese invented
...rossbow sometime
...e 450 B.C. It became one
...e most deadly weapons on
...attlefield. Before an infantry
...e, an army's crossbowmen would
...pt the enemy ranks with a terrifying
...f bolts, which were short, heavy arrows.
...rossbow eventually made the chariot
...ss because its bolts could be fired at the
...y from a safe distance. This ended the
...ce of daring chariot raids.

CHARIOT DECORATION
This magnificent bull's head is
an ornament from the shaft of a
chariot. Elaborately decorated
chariots remained in fashion
long after their usefulness on
the battlefield was over. As a
weapon of war, the chariot was
all but abandoned in the
centuries before the unification
of China in 221 B.C.

*Bronze bull's head
inlaid with gold
and silver*

BIRD-SHAPED HALBERD
A halberd was a bronze blade
carried by foot soldiers. It was often
attached to a long bamboo pole,
which allowed it to be swung at the
enemy from a distance. Such a
weapon could cause great damage.
A halberdier always rode in a
chariot in order to protect the horses
from enemy
infantrymen. The
halberd was the
chief weapon of
war in this period.

*Halberd
would have been
attached to a pole*

Axe blade

*...d decorated
...terlaced dragons*

*Axehead, 6th–5th
century* B.C.

AXEHEAD
Hand-to-hand combat
settled the outcome of
most Chinese battles.
The soldiers of Qin,
who placed the First
Emperor on the throne,
were renowned for
their fearlessness in battle. Once fighting
had started, the Qin infantrymen would
throw off their armour so that they could
swing their axes and halberds more easily.

*Bronze halberd
and ferrule, 4th–3rd
century* B.C.

*Ferrule
would
have been
fixed to
bottom
of weapon
pole*

The first emperor of China

Jade dragon ornaments; the dragon was the adopted symbol of the First Emperor

In 221 B.C. THE CHINESE EMPIRE was formed. The Qin soldiers defeated the last of their enemies and united the "warring states" under one leader, Zheng. To show his supremacy over the kings he had vanquished, Zheng took the title of First Sovereign Qin Emperor, or Qin Shi Huangdi. The empire took its name from the Qin (pronounced "Chin") to become China. The First Emperor (221–207 B.C.) seems to have thought he would become immortal. He built an impressive tomb guarded by thousands of life-sized terracotta warriors, probably in the belief that he would remain a powerful man in the afterlife. His brief reign on earth was harsh. He used his subjects as slave labour to build the Great Wall and ruthlessly suppressed anyone who disagreed with him. But after the First Emperor's rule, the Chinese felt that unity was normal.

A CELESTIAL RULER?
The brief reign of the First Emperor left a permanent impression on Chinese society. But he ruled his subjects harshly and his dynasty was overthrown by a peasant rebellion in 207 B.C., just three years after his death.

THE TERRACOTTA ARMY
The ghostly army of terracotta soldiers, left, that guards the First Emperor's tomb is accompanied by life-size horses and chariots. No two soldiers have the same face – each is an individual portrait of a soldier from the Qin army. The soldiers once carried real weapons, but these were stolen by grave robbers after the fall of the Qin.

Clouds

Dragon roundel, probably used on a 19th-century imperial robe

WHAT'S IN A NAME
This is the beginning of an inscription celebrating the unification of China by the First Emperor in 221 B.C. The top character is part of the First Emperor's title. It conveys the idea of divinity, divine favour

THE BURNING OF THE BOOKS
When scholars disagreed with his harsh acts, the First Emperor burned their books and executed those who spoke against him, as seen above. He was particularly displeased with followers of Confucius who pointed out how his policies differed from the ways of old. In 213 B.C., his chief minister announced: "No one is to use the past to discredit the present." Only books on agriculture, medicine, and oracles were spared the flames.

Waves

THE DRAGON KING
The association of Chinese emperors with the dragon was undoubtedly due to the First Emperor. The dragon became the First Emperor's emblem because it was divine lord of water, the lucky element of his people, the Qin.

GREAT BUILDING WORKS
The First Emperor used the forced labour of his subjects to carry out his extensive public works. These included the Great Wall, roads, and canals. The hardship suffered by the thousands of men who toiled on the Great Wall is still recalled in Chinese folksongs. To fund his projects, the First Emperor taxed his subjects heavily, which led to widespread suffering and starvation.

THE GREAT WALL OF CH
The First Emperor's grea achievement was the constru of the Great Wall in about 214
It joined together a numbe defensive walls aimed at keep out the Xiongnu nomads. It i longest structure ever b

DRAGON CHARACTERISTICS

Chinese dragon has the head of a
[ca]mel, the horns of a stag, the eyes
[of] a demon, the scales of a fish,
[the] claws of an eagle, the pads
[of] a tiger, the ears of a bull,
[and] the long whiskers
[of] a cat. It can make
[its]elf as small as a
[sil]kworm or large
[en]ough to
[ov]ershadow
[th]e world.

Scaly skin

Stag-like horns

Fierce eyes

Long
whiskers

[Cl]ouds

Pearl of
wisdom

The five-clawed
dragon was the
symbol of the
emperor

[TH]E
[IM]PERIAL
[DR]AGON
[Pa]radoxically,
[the] First Emperor
[cho]se a benevolent
[dr]agon as his
[fav]oured deity. The
[Ch]inese dragon, or
[lun]g, is not a terrifying
[mo]nster but a benign
[cre]ature that embodies
[wi]sdom, strength, and goodness.
[Ab]ove all, the dragon symbolizes
[the] life-giving force of water. The
[an]cient Chinese believed that dragons
[inh]abited every river, lake, and sea and also
[soar]ed high in the sky among the rainclouds.

Imperial seal with a
dragon surrounded
by clouds guarding
the pearl of wisdom,
14th century

17

In the empire's service

THE EARLIEST MEMBERS of the imperial civil service were recruited by Gaozu (206–195 B.C.), the first Han emperor. Gaozu led one of the peasant armies that overthrew the Qin dynasty in 207 B.C. Although Gaozu was uneducated, when he came to power he realized the empire needed educated administrators. He gathered together scholars to form an imperial civil service, which was destined to run China for 2,000 years. In 124 B.C. the Han emperor Wu Di (140–87 B.C.) introduced examinations for civil servants and founded an imperial university where candidates studied the ancient Confucian classics. In later dynasties, a series of examinations took successful candidates from their local districts, through the provinces, to the imperial palace. Those who passed the top palace examinations could expect to be appointed as ministers or even marry princesses.

THE MOMENT OF TRUTH
These local magistrates are taking part in a civil service examination. At each level, only a few candidates passed. They answered questions on the Confucian classics, whose 431, 286 words had to be learned by heart. Reform of the curriculum was strongly opposed and it hardly changed through the centuries.

Long beard associated with old age and wisdom

18th-century figure in official garb

19TH-CENTURY EXAM PAPER
This test paper shows a candidate's answer and his tutor's comments. Those who studied for an official career knew it involved long years of preparation, but the rewards were great. On receiving his results, an 8th-century graduate called Meng Jiao remarked: "The drudgery of yesterday is forgotten. Today the prospects are vast, and my heart is filled with joy!"

A WISE OFFICIAL
Qiu Jun, above, was a Ming official who persuaded the emperor to strengthen the Great Wall against the Manchus. His advice was well-founded. The Manchus invaded China in 1644.

Circles indicate praise for calligraphy

THE PASSING OUT PARADE
The special slate or document held by this official would have been carried on formal occasions, such as the splendid graduation ceremony of successful examination candidates. In the imperial palace, top graduates received their degrees and bowed to the emperor.

A NEW CURRICULUM
The Song minister Wang Anshi, above, altered the civil service examinations so that a mastery of technical subjects would be favoured over learning by heart. This reform lasted only briefly.

Plaque was sewn on to official robes

OFFICIAL PLAQUE

...s beautiful gold plaque ...ecorated with imperial ...-clawed dragons and ...ni-precious stones. Such ...xpensive badge of rank ...ly have been worn by an ...perial minister or a prince ...ring the Ming dynasty.

THE DANGERS OF CHEATING
This handkerchief covered with model exam answers would have made a clever crib. However, cheating in the imperial examinations was not only difficult, but dangerous. Candidates sat the provincial examinations in open-doored cells inside walled compounds. Soldiers in watchtowers made sure that no cribs were smuggled in. When the emperor Xian Feng learned of cheating in the palace examinations of 1859, he beheaded the examiners responsible for the cheating, banished the administrators, and took away the qualifications of the guilty graduates.

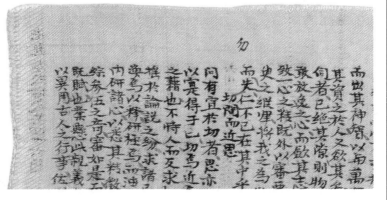

19

Continued on next page

The three ways

IN IMPERIAL CHINA, RELIGIOUS BELIEFS were divided into the "three ways" of Confucianism, Daoism, and Buddhism. Throughout its long history, China was tolerant of all religions. Although there were disagreements over religious principles, few people were persecuted for their beliefs. In this respect, the Chinese empire was unique among civilizations. Confucianism and Daoism emerged in the Warring States period. Against the backdrop of constant warfare, these two religions encouraged more peaceful ways of being. Buddhism came to China from India in the 1st century A.D., and its gentle teachings became popular in the troubled centuries that followed the end of the Han dynasty. The return of strong government under the Tang emperors (618–906) led to the decline of Buddhism and the revival of Confucianism. Nevertheless, Buddhism had become firmly rooted in Chinese culture and became China's most popular belief.

Lao Zi always depicted an old m...

LAO ZI
Daoists were followers of Lao Zi, or the "Old Philosopher" (born c. 604 B.C.), who believed tha[t] people should live in harmony wi[th] nature. He explained his ideas in a book called the *Daodejing*. Lao Zi wanted people to lead simple live[s] that did not disrupt the balance of the natural world. He disliked the importance Confucius placed on duty to family and state because he did not believe in rules and regulations. Daoism was represented by the yin yang sign, which reflects natural harmony.

Zhongli Quan, chief of the eight immortals, who could raise the dead with a wave of his fan

Tortoise, a symbol of luck and wisdom

Sacred scroll

Fan

Flute

THE GENTLE PROTECTOR
Kuanyin was the Buddhist goddess of mercy. Her name means "She Who Hears Prayers", and she is often portrayed as the protector of children. Kuanyin was a Chinese transformation of the Indian male god Avalokitesvara. This is just one of the many changes the Chinese made to Indian Buddhism. In China, Kuanyin was the greatest Buddhist deity.

THE HEIGHT OF BEAUTY
A pagoda is a sacred Buddhist tower. Pagodas have from three to 15 tiers and are usually exquisitely decorated. The Chinese believed that a pagoda brought good fortune to the area surrounding it.

Zhang Guolao an immortal who could make himself invisible

THE MYSTERIES OF THE IMMORTALS
Daoists thought that it was possible to discover the elixir of life and become immortal. They worshipped eight figures whom they believed had achieved immortality. These mysterious immortals, or *xian*, lived in remote mountains. They were said to have supernatural powers, such as the power to turn objects into gold, become invisible, make flowers bloom instantly, or raise the dead.

Han Xiang[g], patron of musici[ans] who could make flow[ers] blossom insta[ntly]

Ivory figures, Ming dynasty, 16th–17th cent[ury]

A GUARDIAN FROM THE SPIRIT WORLD

A Bodhisattva, or "Enlightened Being", is a kind of Buddhist god. Bodhisattvas were said to have postponed their own hope of eternal peace, or nirvana, in order to help other people. Kuanyin, the goddess of mercy, was the greatest Chinese Bodhisattva, but there were many others that Buddhists could call upon when they needed help.

Stucco head of a Bodhisattva, 8th–9th century A.D.

Crown

ONFUCIUS

e great Chinese thinker
onfucius (551–479 B.C.)
ught people to show
spect for one another.
 said that a good ruler
ould cherish his subjects
d they should honour
m. He also believed that
spect within the family was
ry important because a
ble society was based on
ong families. The Daoists did
t agree with Confucius. In his
n defence Confucius said: "They
slike me because I want to reform
ciety, but if we are not to live with
r fellow men with whom can we
e? We cannot live with animals.
 society was as it ought to be, I
ould not seek to change it."

odern Buddhist
age for
mestic use

Auriole shows the emanation of holiness from the Buddha

Buddha seated on a sacred lotus

UDDHA

ddhists follow the teachings of
uddha (born c. 563 B.C.), a north Indian
ince who devoted his life to a search for
rsonal peace, or enlightenment. His name
eans "Enlightened One". Buddha believed that by
ving up worldly desires, such as good food and fine
othes, a blissful state called nirvana could be achieved.
 nirvana there was freedom from the sorrows of the world.
dian belief at that time held that people were reborn many
mes. If a person had lived badly in former lives, they might be
born in animal or insect form. Buddha said that by reaching
rvana, this endless cycle of rebirth could be broken.

Head blends male and female characteristics

27

Health and medicine

TRADITIONAL CHINESE MEDICINE is based on the use of herbs, acupuncture, and a balanced diet. It combines ancient philosophy with practical skills. According to Chinese belief, a person falls ill when the two opposing forces of yin and yang become unbalanced in the body. Doctors use acupuncture and herbal remedies to re-channel these natural energies. Chinese interest in medicine dates back over 4,000 years. In ancient times, the Daoists believed that it was possible to find the elixir of life, which would make people immortal. Concern with health also came from the need to produce strong sons who would ensure the survival of the family. From the Tang dynasty onwards, Chinese doctors were regularly examined on their medical expertise. In 1111, the entire knowledge of the medical profession was compiled in a vast encyclopedia. This great work listed all the known diseases, with their symptoms, diagnoses, and treatments. It became the standard reference book for Chinese medicine.

Liquorice root, or *gan cao*

Chinese hawthorn, or *shan zha*

Smoked plums, or *wu mei*

VITAL NOURISHMENT
The Chinese have always believe a balanced diet to be the basis c good health. The ingredients above make up a nourishing herbal drink said to improve th appetite and clear the chest.

Coin sword from the Qing dynasty, placed by the bed of a sick person to ward off bad spirits

10th-century acupuncture chart showing some of the main needle points in the arm

TAPPING THE LIFE FORCE
Acupuncture has been used to treat illnesses for over 2,000 years. It is based on the belief that the life force of the body flows along 12 lines, or meridians. Each meridian is linked to a different organ in the body. An acupuncturist inserts needles at various points along these meridians to relieve pain or treat illness.

Cap screws securely into case

Set of eight steel acupuncture needles, Qing dynasty

NATURAL PAIN RELIEF
This set of needles belonged to a 19th-century acupuncturist. In the 20th century, doctors discovered that acupuncture could be used as an anaesthetic for surgery. When acupuncture is used during an operation, the patient remains conscious and feels little or no pain. Scientists believe acupuncture works by stimulating the release of endorphins, the brain's natural painkillers.

HEAT TREATMENT
Moxibustion is a pain-relief treatment that uses heat produced by burning dried mugwort, or *moxa*. Acupuncture and moxibustion are often used together. An acupuncture needle can be fitted with a small cap in which *moxa* is burned. The heat is carried into the body by the needle. Burning *moxa* sticks can also be used to apply heat to certain parts of the body.

Moxa stick

Moxa wool

Moxa *burned in cap*

Mahogany case for storing needles

Modern acupuncture needles with a cap for *moxa* wool

Lighted end of moxa *stick is held over painful area*

手厥陰心包經之圖 九九穴 左右二十八穴

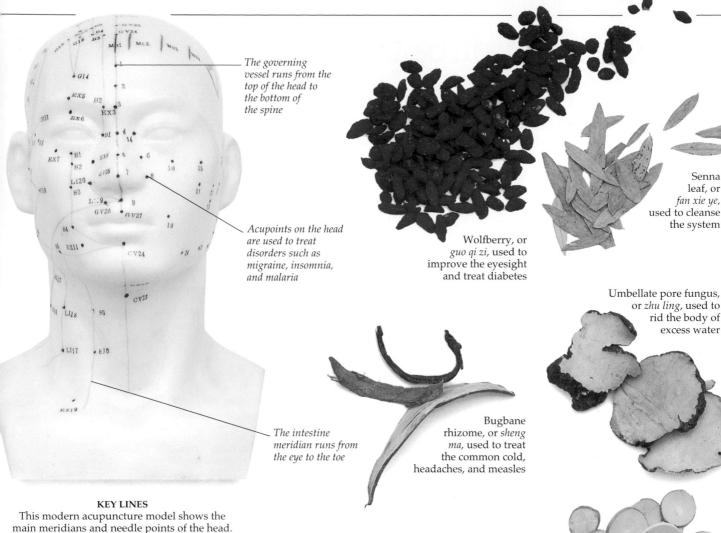

The governing vessel runs from the top of the head to the bottom of the spine

Acupoints on the head are used to treat disorders such as migraine, insomnia, and malaria

The intestine meridian runs from the eye to the toe

KEY LINES
This modern acupuncture model shows the main meridians and needle points of the head. Although 650 different needle points in the body are known, today only around 450 are used. Chinese doctors use acupuncture to treat a variety of conditions, such as arthritis, asthma, migraine, stomach ulcers, and poor eyesight.

Wolfberry, or *guo qi zi*, used to improve the eyesight and treat diabetes

Senna leaf, or *fan xie ye*, used to cleanse the system

Umbellate pore fungus, or *zhu ling*, used to rid the body of excess water

Bugbane rhizome, or *sheng ma*, used to treat the common cold, headaches, and measles

Mulberry wood, or *shang zhi*, used to reduce high blood pressure and relieve rheumatic pain

Chinese yam, or *shan yao*, used to treat fatigue and lack of appetite

Euryale seed, or *qian shi*, used to treat urinary problems

Teasel root, or *xu duan*, used to make an ointment that soothes rheumatic pain and helps broken bones to heal

lberry, *sang shen*, used medicines for er ear problems l dizziness

Chain fern bark, or *gou ji*, used to relieve stiffness and lower back pain

HEALING HERBS
Medicinal herbs such as these have been used in China for thousands of years. In the 16th century, a doctor named Li Shizhen listed an amazing 1,892 herbs and 11,000 prescriptions in a book called the *Bencao Gangmu*. In China, herbs are used not just to treat ailments, but also in home cooking to ensure the good health of the family. Herbs are usually cooked in nutritious soups. The benefits of this kind of preventative medicine are summed up by an unknown Chinese poet who said: "Delicious dishes banish tablets and pills, Nourishing food is the drug for all ills."

The three perfections

CALLIGRAPHY, POETRY, AND PAINTING were known as the "three perfections". The combination of these arts was considered the height of artistic expression. They were usually combined in the form of a poetically inspired landscape painting with beautiful calligraphy running down one side. From the Song dynasty (960–1279) onwards, the practice of the three perfections was seen as the greatest accomplishment of an educated person. The Song emperor Hui Zong (1101–25) led the way towards transforming writing into an art form. He developed an elegant style of calligraphy called "slender gold". Hui Zong was also a gifted poet and painter, and the arts flourished under his reign.

IN THE BEGINNING
Legend has it that Chinese writing was invented over 4,000 years ago by Cang Jie, an official of the mythical Yellow Emperor. He devised written characters from the tracks of birds and animals. The legend says that "all the spirits cried out in agony, as the innermost secrets of nature were revealed".

Water well to dip ink stick into

THE DAILY GRIND
Calligraphers produced their own ink by grinding ink sticks or cakes into a small amount of water on an inkstone. Inkstones were made from stone or pottery. Smooth, hard stones were favoured because they allowed the ink to be finely ground to make smooth ink. This inkstone from the Qing dynasty is made from Duan stone and carved in the shape of two fungi.

Soft, springy brush tip probably made from wolf hair

Ink stick is rubbed on the smooth part of the inkstone

Ink cake decorated with a legendary animal

Classical garden depicted in mother-of-pearl inlay

Box lined with tortoiseshell

CARBON COPY
Ink was made by mixing pine soot with lampblack obtained from other burned plants. This mixture was combined with glue and moulded into a stick or cake. Ink sticks and cakes were often decorated with calligraphy or moulded into the shapes of dragons and birds copied from mythology.

19th-century ink box

A TREASURED POSSESSION
This beautiful writing brush from the Ming dynasty is made from lacquered wood and inlaid with mother-of-pearl. It was usual for everyday writing implements to be highly decorated. In the 10th century the brushes, paper, ink, and inkstone used by a calligrapher became known as "the four treasures of the scholar's studio".

COLOURED INKS
Both calligraphers and painters used inks. In the Song dynasty, coloured inks were made by adding materials such as pearl powder, ground jade, and camphor to ink. Later other pigments were used: indigo for blue, lead for white, cinnabar for red, and malachite for green.

Modern coloured ink sticks embossed with gold dragons

The character
[...]ns "brilliant";
[...]mes from a
[...] composed
[...]und 1120

[...] stroke
[...]t be drawn
[...]refully
[...] in the
[...] order

DROP BY DROP
This Ming bronze water dropper is in the shape of a boy riding a buffalo. A water dropper was used for wetting the inkstone. It was important to control the supply of water mixed with an ink stick because this affected the tone of the ink. A Tang landscape painter noted that "five colours can be obtained from black ink alone". Calligraphers and painters often had assistants to help prepare ink while they were working.

*Seal-paste box,
19th century*

Seal

Impression

A GOOD IMPRESSION
Many scholars used a seal as a way of identifying their work. A seal would identify its owner either directly by name or with a favourite quotation. Seal impressions were always printed in red ink. Special paintings might end up covered with different impressions as later admirers and owners affixed their seals to the work.

*Calligrapher
awaits
inspiration*

BOLD AND BRILLIANT
This is an example of the elegant "slender gold" calligraphy of the Song emperor Hui Zong. For a calligrapher, style was as important as accuracy.

PRACTICE MAKES PERFECT
To become a good calligrapher requires years of practice. Because Chinese writing is based on signs rather than sounds, every sign, or character, must be learned by heart. The strokes that make up each character must be written in the correct sequence. With over 40,000 characters in the Chinese language, the calligrapher's art is not an easy one.

NATURAL BEAUTY
This stoneware brush washer from the 18th century is made in the form of a lotus pod. Scholars were uplifted by the beauty of natural forms.

*Brush rest in the
shape of a three-
peaked mountain*

CELESTIAL INSPIRATION
The production of ornamental ink cakes became a minor art form. This octagonal ink cake is decorated with a celestial horse carrying sacred Daoist writings. It was made in 1621 by a famous Ming ink-cake manufacturer called Cheng Dayue. By the time of the Ming dynasty, all educated Chinese people felt they should be skilled in the art of either calligraphy or painting.

PAUSE FOR THOUGHT
A brush rest was an essential item for a calligrapher or painter. This dainty enamel brush rest would have been placed on a writing table. A calligrapher may have placed his writing brush upon it while he awaited inspiration.

Continued on next page

The poetry of landscapes

The soft inks and delicate brushstrokes used in calligraphy were also applied to painting. In the Song dynasty, this technique was used to great effect in the painting of landscapes. Inks created moody, evocative images. For "wet" works that depicted rolling mists or stormy clouds, artists brushed ink washes on to special absorbent paper. The Song emperor Hui Zong added painting to the subjects set in the top civil service examinations. The examination question quoted a line of poetry that had to be illustrated in an original way. Scholars often joined together to demonstrate the three artistic "perfections". One might paint a scene, and another would add a line of poetry in stylish calligraphy.

OFFICIAL POETS
The Song official Su Shi, right, was a famous poet. Many officials were accomplished writers of poetry and prose. Those that studied together were often posted to opposite ends of the empire, but they continued to exchange calligraphy and verse. Their correspondence counts for a great mass of Chinese literature.

The brush tip contains several different layers of hair

The inner core of hairs is often waxed to make the brush tip springy

AN EMPEROR'S POEM
This delicate jade bowl stand is carved in the shape of a *bi*, a disc used in ancient rituals. It is inscribed with a poem by the Manchu, or Qing emperor Qianlong. In the inscription, the emperor says that his "poetic imagination" was stirred by the "subtle and exquisite" shape of the bowl stand and the quality of the jade from which it is made. The foreign emperor Qianlong was a great admirer of Chinese art and collected poems, paintings, and calligraphy from the length and breadth of his empire.

High-quality jade

Goat hair tip

Buffalo horn handle

Carved dragon curls around the pot

Modern Chinese calligraphy brushes for writing large characters

A JADE BRUSH WASHER
The feeling of harmony inspired by classical forms and designs was important to the Chinese scholar. Even the humblest objects in a scholar's studio were lovely to look at. This exquisite jade pot was actually used for washing brushes! It is carved with dragons, a favourite Chinese motif, and dates from the Ming dynasty.

Pine tree

Scholar deep in thought

A TRANQUIL SETTING
The scene carved on this 17th-century bamboo brush pot represents a Chinese ideal – a scholar seated quietly underneath a pine tree admiring the beauty of nature.

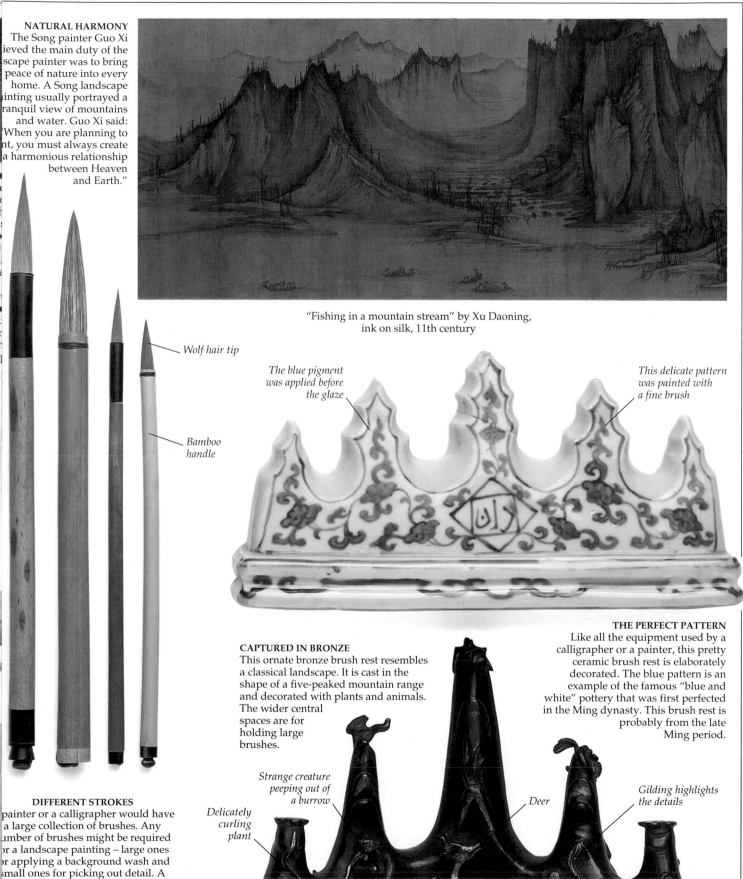

NATURAL HARMONY

The Song painter Guo Xi believed the main duty of the landscape painter was to bring the peace of nature into every home. A Song landscape painting usually portrayed a tranquil view of mountains and water. Guo Xi said: "When you are planning to paint, you must always create a harmonious relationship between Heaven and Earth."

"Fishing in a mountain stream" by Xu Daoning,
ink on silk, 11th century

Wolf hair tip

Bamboo handle

The blue pigment was applied before the glaze

This delicate pattern was painted with a fine brush

DIFFERENT STROKES

A painter or a calligrapher would have a large collection of brushes. Any number of brushes might be required for a landscape painting – large ones for applying a background wash and small ones for picking out detail. A professional calligrapher might need a brush with hair over half a metre long for writing big characters on banners and posters. Brushes were carefully made for these purposes. The hairs of a brush tip could be constructed to produce a soft wash, a firm and even stroke, or a lively, flamboyant line.

CAPTURED IN BRONZE

This ornate bronze brush rest resembles a classical landscape. It is cast in the shape of a five-peaked mountain range and decorated with plants and animals. The wider central spaces are for holding large brushes.

Strange creature peeping out of a burrow

Delicately curling plant

Deer

THE PERFECT PATTERN

Like all the equipment used by a calligrapher or a painter, this pretty ceramic brush rest is elaborately decorated. The blue pattern is an example of the famous "blue and white" pottery that was first perfected in the Ming dynasty. This brush rest is probably from the late Ming period.

Gilding highlights the details

Seeds and ploughshares

Traditionally peasant farmers used ancient methods of farming which involved hoeing their crops by hand, transporting water by bucket, and grinding grain with manually operated mills. In the Han dynasty, wealthy farmers built bigger, labour-saving machines powered by water or animals. Iron ploughshares pulled by oxen, new irrigation machines, and watermills greatly improved farming output. However, small farmers still relied on human labour. By the Song dynasty, new crop strains and knowledge of fertilizers allowed the peasant farmers in southern China to grow two crops a year in the same field.

REMOVING THE HUSKS
This hand-powered winnowing machine was used to separate the outer shells, or husks, from the grain. Winnowing was traditionally carried out by shaking the grain in a large sieve, then tossing it in the air to remove the husks.

THE HUMAN HAMMER
Harvested grain was crushed by a tilt-hammer. This machine was powered by a single man who used weight to tilt the hammer backwards and forwards in a see-saw action. There were larger, water-driven tilt-hammers in mills near towns and cities.

PLANTING OUT A PADDY FIELD
These peasant farmers are transplanting young rice plants in the soft mud of a paddy field. Originally rice was grown only in flooded paddies, but later farmers cultivated rice in dry fields in areas supplied with a good rainfall.

ALL HANDS TO THE HARVEST
This painting from the Yuan dynasty shows a group of peasant farmers harvesting rice. In rural communities, everyone helped with the farm work and women laboured alongside men in the fields. Peasant women never had their feet bound because they would have been unable to carry out any kind of field work.

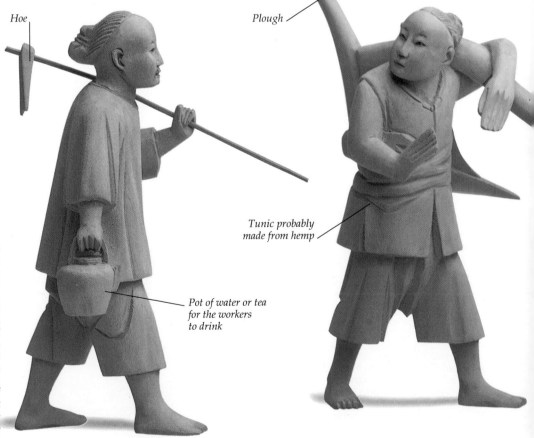

PLOUGHING THE LAND
During the Han dynasty, government iron foundries began producing ploughshares. They were made in various sizes, from large ploughshares that were pulled by an oxen team to small, pointed ones that could be used by a single person. According to an ancient Chinese proverb, farmers should always plough their land after rain to conserve the moisture in the ground. The new iron equipment made this back-breaking task much easier.

Hoe

Plough

Tunic probably made from hemp

A LITTLE HELP FROM SOME FRIENDS
This 19th-century model depicts a group of peasant farmers going off to plough their fields. Although every rural family had to support itself, co-operation with friends and neighbours was essential. The upkeep of irrigation ditches and the repair of terraces were tasks shared by the whole village. Larger enterprises were organized by local government. In 111 B.C., the Han emperor Wu Di said: "Agriculture is the basic occupation of the world. So the imperial government must cut canals and ditches, guide the rivers, and build reservoirs in order to prevent flood and drought."

Pot of water or tea for the workers to drink

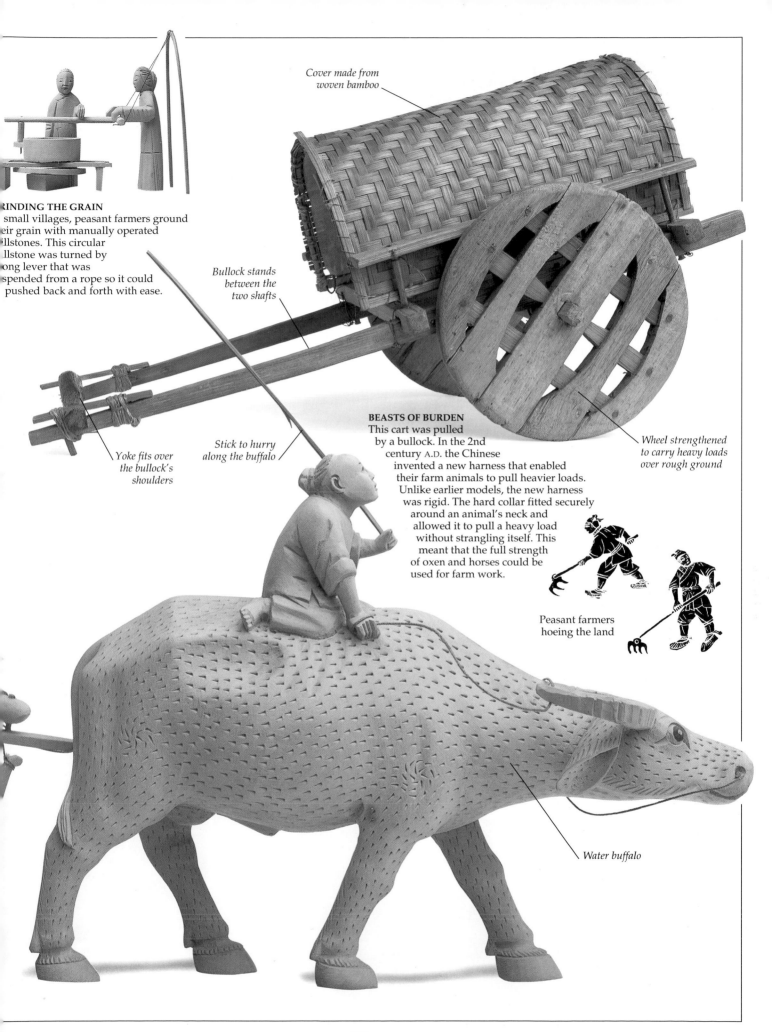

Cover made from
woven bamboo

GRINDING THE GRAIN
In small villages, peasant farmers ground
their grain with manually operated
millstones. This circular
millstone was turned by
a long lever that was
suspended from a rope so it could
be pushed back and forth with ease.

Bullock stands
between the
two shafts

Yoke fits over
the bullock's
shoulders

Stick to hurry
along the buffalo

BEASTS OF BURDEN
This cart was pulled
by a bullock. In the 2nd
century A.D. the Chinese
invented a new harness that enabled
their farm animals to pull heavier loads.
Unlike earlier models, the new harness
was rigid. The hard collar fitted securely
around an animal's neck and
allowed it to pull a heavy load
without strangling itself. This
meant that the full strength
of oxen and horses could be
used for farm work.

Wheel strengthened
to carry heavy loads
over rough ground

Peasant farmers
hoeing the land

Water buffalo

37

Within the city walls

Circular end-tile

Lookout

KEEPING A LOOK-OUT
This pottery model of a watchtower dates from the Han dynasty. Watchtowers were common in Chinese towns and cities because the authorities kept a strict eye on the inhabitants.

THE LANDSCAPE OF IMPERIAL CHINA was dotted with walled towns and cities. These enclosed urban communities were centres of government and the power of the authorities was reinforced by town planning. Towns and cities were traditionally built on a grid system and divided into sections called wards. Each ward was surrounded by walls with gates that were locked every evening. Drums sounded from a central tower to warn inhabitants when the gates were closing, and often visiting friends or relatives would have to stay overnight. In general, wealthy people and government officials lived at one end of a town or city and the poor at the other. Markets were usually situated along one of the main streets. In the later years of the Chinese empire, towns and cities were built on a less rigid structure. However, citizens were always firmly under the control of the authorities. A French resident of 18th-century Beijing reported: "The police know all that is going on, even inside the palaces of the princes. They keep exact registers of the inhabitants of every house."

COUNTING THE COST
Towns and cities were centres of trade and commerce. Local peasant farmers brought their produce to market and also their grain-tax to be collected by officials. Large transactions may have been carried out with the aid of an abacus such as this one. The exact origin of this helpful calculating device is unknown, but it was certainly in common use by the Ming dynasty.

ON THE TILES
Traditional Chinese buildings were protected by heavy, overhanging tile roofs. In Chinese belief, a roof was a safeguard against bad spirits as well as harsh weather. Roof tiles were often decorated with symbols and inscriptions to ward off evil influences.

The dragon is a good luck symbol

Pottery roof tiles, Ming dynasty

DRUMMING UP TRADE
This pellet-drum was used to attract customers. Street vendors had their own sounds to announce their presence and advertise their wares.

Cup for ladling out food

STREET TRADE
This man is selling food. Hawkers wandered the streets of every Chinese town or city selling cooked and uncooked foods. The main streets were lined with market stalls that sold all kinds of produce. People could buy special dishes from stallholders to take home for family meals.

A pellet-drum was held in the hand and twirled from side to side

...tery
...f ornament
...m a palace
...f, Ming
...nasty

...OF GUARDIAN
...s yellow pottery
...st was placed at
...end of a roof ridge.
...ythical beasts like this
...re intended to act as
...ardians. Official buildings
...d the houses of wealthy people
...re often highly ornamented with
...corated tiles and pottery figures.

...llow roof
...s were used
...important
...ildings

Classical pagoda

Platform

Overhanging tile roof

TRADITIONAL ARCHITECTURE
Chinese buildings were raised above the damp ground on platforms of rammed earth, brick, or stone. Their heavy, overhanging roofs were supported by a structure of sturdy wooden beams, which allowed for movement in an earthquake.

Traditional Chinese buildings, Ming dynasty

CITY WALL
This European engraving shows the strong walls surrounding a city. Traditionally the walls of towns and cities were built in a square shape, which symbolized the four corners of the Earth. It was important for the Chinese to feel that they were in tune with nature. The site for a new town or city was carefully chosen using cosmological calculations to make sure that its position was a favourable one.

Pottery roof tiles, Ming dynasty

Food and drink

Court ladies
enjoying a banquet,
Tang dynasty

IN CHINA, THE ART OF COOKING has been celebrated since early times. Feasts formed an important part of Chinese life and wealthy people often enjoyed elaborate banquets. In contrast, for most of the year ordinary people lived on a simple diet of pulses and vegetables, with very little meat. Though rice was always the favourite staple food in China, people in the northern provinces ate mainly millet and some wheat. Both rich and poor Chinese flavoured their food with a wide variety of herbs and spices. To save fuel, food was chopped into small pieces and cooked quickly in an iron frying pan, or *wok*, for a few minutes only. Many foods were also steamed or stewed. Today Chinese food is enjoyed throughout the world.

A sharp knife,
the main tool of
a Chinese cook

Chopstic

Case for
chopstick and
knife set

TEA CONNOISSEURS
Tea, or *cha*, has been grown in China since the 2nd century B.C. By the Tang dynasty, tea-making had become a fine art. These Yuan-dynasty tea merchants are taking part in a tea-tasting competition. As experts, they would be able to tell apart the many delicately flavoured varieties of Chinese tea.

NATURALLY PRESERVED
The Chinese preserved much of their food by drying it in the sun, and dried ingredients are common in Chinese cookery. After soaking in cold water, this dried cuttlefish can be used to flavour a stir-fried dish.

Song-dynasty tea
bowls, 12th
century

TIME FOR TEA
In Tang times, boiled water was poured from a ewer into small bowls containing powdered tea. The bowls rested on lacquer bowl stands. In the 13th century, people began to steep loose leaves in hot water, and the teapot came into use. Today, many kinds of tea are grown, but the drying method produces three main types: black (which can be red or coppery in colour), oolong (amber), and green. Leaves are often chopped and blended, and some teas contain flowers. The tea shown on the right is called gunpowder tea because its leaves are rolled into balls that resemble lead shot.

Peanuts, eaten as a tasty
snack or added to
cooked dishes

*Tea leaves
unfurl when
soaked in water*

CHOPSTICKS
In China, food is slice
into thin slivers befor
cooking, so people do r
need to use knives to c
up their food when the
are eating. Instead, th
Chinese use chopstick
to pick up morsels
of food from small
porcelain bowls.

Porcelain bowl,
18th century

Peas,
often ground
into flour

Mung
beans, eaten as
a sweet or a
savoury

*A china bowl
preserves the
taste of food*

Soya beans,
processed into curd,
milk, dried sticks,
or soya sauce

Wheat, often used to
make dumplings

Soya bean curd, or *doufu*
(tofu), can be steamed,
boiled, or fried

Rice, used to make
wine as well as cakes
and puddings

A STAPLE DIET
Rice was grown mainly in the
southern Chinese provinces, but with
improved transportation, it became the
favourite staple food throughout China. Millet
and wheat were the chief crops grown in the
north, but wheat never formed a staple part of
the Chinese diet as it did in Europe and America.
Beans were an important source of protein for
the Chinese – soya beans contain more
protein than any other plant or animal food.

THE SPICE OF LIFE
The Chinese have always relished different
tastes and flavours. Chinese cooks became
expert at blending herbs and spices to create
sweet, sour, bitter, hot, or salty tastes.
Seasoning was important to ordinary people
because much of their basic diet consisted of
quite bland food. Soya beans were fermented
to make tasty soya sauce, and more delicate
flavours were derived from ingredients such as
flower petals and tangerine peel.

Chili peppers,
traditionally
added to hot,
spicy dishes
in south-
western China

Star aniseed, a
popular spice
native to
China

Ginger, originally
used to disguise the
odour of old meat

Sesame seeds,
sprinkled on
both sweet and
savoury foods

odles,
de from wheat,
n, or rice flour

Dressed for best

THE CLOTHES OF RICH AND POOR Chinese were very different. Peasant farmers wore loose garments made usually of hemp, a rough fabric woven from plant fibres. Members of the imperial court, wealthy ladies, high-ranking officials, and scholars wore splendid robes of fine silk. This luxurious material was reserved exclusively for the use of these privileged groups. In some dynasties, rich merchants who traded in silk were forbidden from wearing it themselves, and many were punished for wearing fine silk beneath their outer garments. The supply of materials used for making clothes was protected by imperial decree. Both hemp and silk cloth were stockpiled in government storehouses in case of shortages. Towards the end of the empire, cotton became popular, but it never replaced silk as a luxury fabric.

PERSONAL GROOMING
Beauty treatment was always a matter of concern for the well-born Chinese lady. The eyebrows received special attention. They were plucked with tweezers and were usually enhanced by painting as well.

Tweezer and ear scoop set

Scoop for cleaning the ears

Tweezers

Bronze tweezers used for eyebrow plucking

Three pairs of tweezers

Tongue scraper

Jade ear scoop

Scoop

Luxurious vermilion-coloured silk

The peony, often called the "king of flowers" because of its large red petals, was a popular decorative motif

The o... segment of the ... is decorated wi... garden sc...

CARVED IVORY FAN
Fans were a favourite item of dress for both men and women in China. This expensive ivory fan is decorated with intricately carved flowers and trees. Cheaper fans were made from bamboo and paper. Their decoration could take the form of a painting or a poem.

Delicate flowers embroidered in silk thread

Platform heel would allow only tiny steps

PLATFORM SHOE
This delicate platform slipper belonged to a Manchu lady. The Manchus ruled China during the Qing dynasty. Unlike wealthy Chinese women, Manchu women did not bind their feet to make them smaller. The Chinese believed that tiny, pointed feet were an essential feature of female beauty, and girls' feet were bound from early childhood. As late as 1902, a Manchu emperor issued an order banning this painful practice.

Silk tassels

SILK TIES
These red silk ankle bands were used for binding on gaiters. The richness of the embroidery shows that they came from the wardrobe of a wealthy lady. Embroidery was common on clothes worn by both men and women of quality. Designs often included good luck symbols or mythological scenes.

Fine silk cloth is
light to wear

Wide sleeve

Miniature
roundel, or
circular
design

toggle
to fasten
robe

butterfly
symbol
y

yellow
s is
cred
nese
er

FLOWING SILK ROBE
The beauty of this 19th-
century silk robe indicates
that it was once worn by a
lady of considerable taste. It
is made from a kind of silk
tapestry called *kesi* in which
the pattern is woven into the
fabric. The wonderful design
of flowers and butterflies is
intended to create the
impression of spring. Along
the hem, the garment is
finished with a traditional
wave border.

*An elaborate roundel,
a design popular
towards the end of
the empire*

*The bat is
an emblem
of good luck*

*The peony
represents
spring*

*Wave
border*

Adornment

For the Chinese, the way people dressed was never a casual matter. Personal ornaments were worn by men and women both as decoration and as a sign of rank. A person's jewellery made it possible to tell at a glance their position in China's rigid social hierarchy. From early times, belt hooks and plaques were the most important items of jewellery for men, while women decorated their elaborate hairstyles with beautiful hairpins and combs. In the later Chinese empire, jewellery became an important part of official costume and the materials used to make it were regulated by law. These rules did not apply to women's jewellery. Wealthy women wore stunning pieces made from gold or silver and set with pearls, precious stones, and kingfisher feathers.

Gold openwork in the "cracked ice" pattern

Nail guard protects the long nail of the little finger

Silver nail guard

NAIL GUARDS
During the final centuries of the empire it was customary for wealthy men and women to grow their little finger nails extremely long as a sign of their rank. Their long nails showed that they did not have to do manual work.

GOLDEN CHA
This lovely gold nec[k] from the Qing dynasty is decora[ted] with lucky, or auspicious, symb[ols]. The symbols were intended to br[ing] the wearer good luck and to w[ard] off evil influences. Even tod[ay] Chinese jewellery has a se[cret] magical purpo[se]

ARMLET
After jade, gold was the most prized material used by Chinese craftsmen. This armlet is made from solid gold coiled into a spiral. It is one of a pair that dates from the Mongol, or Yuan dynasty.

Garment hook shaped like a lute

Intricate inlay of turquoise and gold

Bronze belt hook inlaid with silver

The end of a belt hook fits into a ring or buckle

BY HOOK OR BY CROOK
Belt and garment hooks came into use in China in about the 4th century B.C. They were probably copied from neighbouring tribes such as the Xiongnu nomads. In early China, hooks were made from bronze and were often inlaid with gold, silver, and semi-precious stones. Decorated hooks became an essential part of clothing for Chinese men.

Cicada-shaped belt hook

Decorative dragon

Dragon head

BUCKLE UP
Belt hooks fastened into buckles like these, which were also highly decorated.

The end of the hook pokes through here

Two birds entwined together

WEIGHTY MATT[ERS]
Sleeve weights such as these w[ere] used to weigh down the long, flow[ing] sleeves of ceremonial robes. Th[ey] helped the wide sleeves to ha[ng] properly and kept them from flapp[ing] around. These two bird-shaped sle[eve] weights date from the Tang dyna[sty]. They are made from bronze a[nd] decorated with bright gildi[ng]

Pair of openwork gold hairpins, Tang dynasty

PINNED IN PLACE
Chinese women paid particular attention to their hair. From early times, they wore elaborate hairstyles that were held in place with combs and hairpins. Wealthy women used beautifully decorated hairpins made from gold, silver, jade, and glass.

Group of four gold and silver hairpins, Qing dynasty

The mirror was held or suspended by the central boss

Floral design enhanced with gilding

...nze mirror,
...n dynasty

**...RROR
...AGES**
...the Han
...asty, bronze
...rors were mass-produced
...oughout China. The Chinese believed
...t mirrors represented harmony within
...universe and they were often
...orated with cosmological
...s like this mirror above.
...reverse side was highly
...ished to act as a reflector.

...IR CARE
...s impressive silver comb
...y have belonged to a
...utiful court lady. Fine
...men often underwent
...eral hours of
...rdressing every
...rning. Personal
...ids combed and
...sted their hair
...o the fashionable
...rstyles of the day.

Fine silver prongs

HAIR ORNAMENT
This hollow jade hair ornament fitted over a topknot and was held in place by a hairpin. Chinese women favoured complex hairstyles and hair ornaments were their favourite items of jewellery.

Fruiting vine motif

PRECIOUS GIFTS
During the Han dynasty, the Chinese constantly fought and made peace with the fierce Xiongnu nomads who roamed the lands north of the Great Wall. Peaceful relations were celebrated with the exchange of gifts. The Chinese received decorated belt hooks, plaques, and buckles. These exotic ornaments were widely copied until they became an integral part of Chinese dress.

Griffin attacking a tiger

Peony design moulded on lid

GILDING THE LILY
Well-to-do women enhanced their appearances with cosmetics. This delicate 18th-century cosmetic box contains tiny paint palettes in the shape of a lotus.

Bronze belt plaque, 4th–3rd century B.C.

A SIGN OF SUCCESS
Expensive belt plaques such as this one, left, were often worn by high-ranking officials as a sign of their status. This elegant 14th-century plaque is made from silver and gilt.

MARTIAL JEWELLERY
This gilt bronze belt plaque dates from the 3rd–1st century B.C. It is an example of the kind of belt decoration copied by the Chinese from their warlike nomadic neighbours. The bold design shows two horses fighting. Belt plaques were sewn on to the front of a belt.

Festivals and games

MOST CHINESE PEOPLE WORKED from dawn to dusk every day with no regular days off. However, the Chinese calendar was punctuated by several national festivals. The largest of these was the New Year, which marked the beginning of spring. During this 15-day holiday, family members gathered together to share an elaborate meal and exchange gifts. Another important family festival was the Qingming when people swept clean the graves of their family ancestors and left offerings of food for the ancestral spirits. The little spare time people had was often spent playing dice, card games, or games of skill such as chess. Wealthy people spent their leisure hours practising calligraphy, composing poetry, or listening to music.

FLIGHTS OF FANCY
Kite-flying became a favourite pastime towards the end of the Chinese empire. In the Qing dynasty, an autumn kite festival was introduced by the Manchu emperors. The festival was called Tengkao, which means "Mounting the Height" because people flew kites from high ground. They believed this would bring them good luck. Officials took part in the hope that they might be promoted to a higher rank.

Each different chess piece is identified by name

CHECKMATE
The Chinese adopted the game of chess from Europe, but they already had many board games of their own, such as Chinese chequers.

Chinese chess pieces, 19th century

One player uses red pieces, the other blue

Die shaken inside box before being rolled

A ROLL OF THE DICE
The Chinese loved games of chance, and dice games were played in China from ancient times. These brass boxes and dice were probably used for gambling games.

Smaller box inside large one

CHINESE LANTER[N]
Festivals and special eve[nts] were often illuminated [by] the light of decorat[ed] lanterns. Lanterns w[ere] made from paper, silk, ho[rn] or glass and were sometim[es] painted with pictures [or] calligraphy. The end of [the] New Year was celebra[ted] by the Lantern Festi[val]

IDLE AMUSEMENT
These 19th-century gambling tablets come from the eastern port of Shanghai. Gambling was popular in China, especially among merchants. Because they were barred from all the important positions in society, Chinese merchants spent many of their leisure hours at the gambling table.

Die

A set of seven gambling tablets

The emperor Tai Zu playing football around 965 A.D.

AN IMPER[IAL] CENTRE FORWA[RD]
The Song emperor [Tai] Zu enjoyed play[ing] football w[ith] members of [his] court. Wom[en] also took p[art] in games [of] Chinese footb[all] which involved ski[ll,] ball control and pass[ing] rather than rough tackli[ng]

Long kite is aerodynamically designed to help it stay airborne

HIGH AS A KITE
The Chinese probably invented kites about 3,000 years ago. In the Han dynasty kites were used to frighten the enemy in battle, but later kites were flown to celebrate festivals. Kites were often made in animal shapes and could be very long indeed. This modern kite has a dragon's head and a centipede's body.

QUICK STICKS
Gambling sticks have existed in China for hundreds of years. Games were probably played by shaking the sticks out of a pot on to a table. These kinds of sticks were also used for fortune telling. An expert "read" the first stick shaken out of the container to predict future events.

Seal impression reads: "Offering congratulations on the New Year"

Beautifully carved horned sheep with lambs

SEALED WITH GOOD WISHES
The words of this 18th-century seal extend greetings for the New Year. Seals like this may have been stamped on family correspondence during the New Year period. The New Year festival was a time of family reunion. Every family member made it a special duty to return home to share in feasts and celebrations with their relatives.

PLAYING CARDS
The Chinese invented playing cards, and a large number of card games were developed over the centuries. These cards come from three different packs. There were 30 cards in a standard pack.

Cylindrical bamboo container

Carved jade dragon, Ming dynasty

NEW YEAR DRAGONS
People believed the dragon brought happiness and good fortune, and it embodied the generous spirit of the New Year festival. Good wishes and hospitality were plentiful at the New Year. People visited each other bearing gifts, and young family members paid respects to senior relatives. It was believed that a year of bad luck would plague anyone who turned away a visitor.

Living in harmony

HISTORY IN SONG
In later imperial China, opera was the most popular form of theatre. Operas usually related stories based on great historical events, often with a great deal of humour mixed in. Characters were identified by their vividly painted faces. Traditional Chinese opera is still performed. The scene above is from a production in Shanghai.

IN IMPERIAL CHINA, MUSIC was thought to be an important part of civilized life. At the royal palace, the court orchestra played when the emperor received visitors or held banquets. Beautiful ceremonial music also accompanied religious rituals. Confucius thought music was almost as necessary as food. He believed that playing an instrument, singing, or listening to a suitable musical composition encouraged a sense of inner harmony. On the other hand, he thought that certain kinds of music led to rowdy or violent behaviour, and he condemned these as immoral. As an unknown scholar remarked: "The greatest music is that filled with the most delicate sounds."

Assembled *sheng*

Band to hold pipes together

The *sheng*, seen here in pieces, is made up of 17 pipes

Long, elegant sleeve

Wind chamber and mouth-piece seen from above

Dancer

Mouthpiece

Brass "reeds" create the sound

Finger holes

Harp

AN ANCIENT MOUTH-ORGAN
The *sheng* is a Chinese mouth organ made from bamboo pipes. It is played by blowing into and sucking air from a wind chamber while fingering the holes in the pipes. Several *sheng* were played together. This kind of wind instrument has been in existence in China since ancient times.

Remnants of bright red paint on robe

Strings would have been threaded into model

MUSIC IN THE AFTERLIFE
Since music was considered such an important part of life, models of musicians were often placed in tombs to provide entertainment in the afterlife. This little terracotta orchestra, complete with a dancing girl, was found in a Tang-dynasty tomb. The figures were once painted with bright colours.

Bridge

Perforations
let sound
out of box

oden
aters

Tuning
tool

Tuning pegs

The *yang qin*, or "foreign zither", was a late addition to the Chinese orchestra. It was introduced into China in about the 18th century and soon became popular. The *yang qin* is played by striking the strings with a pair of delicate beaters. Its 14 strings produce a wide range of silvery notes.

Lacquered
board

Bridge

h-century *qin*

Strings are
plucked by hand

THE LYRICAL LUTE
The classical lute, or *qin*, is a kind of Chinese zither with seven strings. The *qin* dates back over 2,000 years, and older designs had up to 20 strings. The music of the *qin* was greatly admired for its gentle, plaintive quality and it was a favourite instrument in imperial China.

Mother-of-pearl
discs indicate
finger positions

Remnants of
blue paint on
headdress

Flute

COURT ORCHESTRA
Many court occasions were accompanied by music. These female musicians are playing various wind and string instruments including the *sheng*, the flute, and the *qin*. The musician in the bottom right-hand corner is playing another popular Chinese instrument, the drum.

Lute

Gardens of Heaven

THE CHINESE LOOKED ON GARDENS as works of art. The main elements of a garden were the same as those of a traditional landscape painting – craggy mountains and still water. These appeared in gardens as outcrops of weatherworn rock and tranquil lakes or ponds. Chinese gardens were designed to reflect nature in other ways. Trees were allowed to grow into interesting gnarled shapes, and plants and flowers were cultivated in natural-looking clumps. The garden was a place for quiet thought and spiritual refreshment. Unexpected features that inspired the imagination were prized, and graceful pavilions and bridges enhanced the impression of natural harmony. Towns and cities were planned to include secluded parks where, as a Ming garden treatise promised, the urban population could find "stillness in the midst of the city turmoil".

NATURE PERFECTED
The natural arrangement of the Chinese garden can be seen in this 19th-century painting of the palace gardens in Beijing. Visitors to these famous landscape gardens felt they were entering a natural paradise. Artificial hills and lakes, bright flowers, elegant pines, and ornamental rocks were creatively assembled to reflect the glories of nature.

Detail from purse decoration

With its sweet song, the cicada was a welcome visitor to the Chinese garden

Lotus-shaped cup carved from horn

SACRED BLOSSOMS
The lotus was regarded as the supreme flower of summer. Its pale blossoms graced the tranquil lakes and pools of many Chinese parks and gardens. The lotus was seen as a symbol of purity and was sacred to both the Buddhist and Daoist religions.

KING OF FLOWERS
The peony symbolized spring. It was known as the "king of flowers" because of its large red petals. Chinese gardeners planted peonies in dense clumps or along walls.

The bright, dancing butterfly was a symbol of joy

Swallowtail butterfly

Peony

NATURE STUDY
This 19th-century purse is beautifully embroidered with a butterfly and a cicada. The Chinese had great respect for such tiny creatures, because Buddhism taught that every living thing had a special value. Gardens were an ideal place for the study of nature. The Song emperor Hui Zong held competitions in the painting of flowers, birds, and insects in the lovely palace gardens of Kaifeng.

THE KINGDOM OF FLOWERS
The Chinese loved flowers, as the floral motif of this embroidered sleeve band shows. China was known as the "Flowery Kingdom". It is the original home of many flowers, trees, and fruits now grown throughout the world. The orange, the tea rose, the plane tree, the rhododendron, and the Chinese gooseberry, which is commonly known as the kiwi fruit, are all native Chinese plants.

FLOWER POWER

Garden plants and flowers were prized for their symbolic value as well as for their natural beauty. The winter plum blossom, for example, symbolized personal renewal, and the tough bamboo plant stood for strength and lasting friendship. These exquisite lacquer boxes from the Ming dynasty are carved with some of China's most popular flowers, including the peony and the chrysanthemum.

TURALLY INSPIRED
rdens were favourite places for literary
etings. These Ming scholars have
hered together in a garden to read and
te poetry. An "ink boy" prepares a
ply of ink to make sure that the
olar who is about to compose
se will not have to interrupt his
v once inspiration strikes.

FRUIT OF PARADISE
The bright red fruit of the lychee tree adorned many gardens in southern China. This attractive fruit was also prized for its juicy white flesh.

LASTING BEAUTY
The chrysanthemum was the flower of autumn. It was esteemed for the variety and richness of its colours. Because it outlasted the frost, the chrysanthemum was adopted as the Chinese symbol for long life.

FLOWER OF FORTUNE
The narcissus was a favourite New Year flower. The opening of its delicate buds was thought to bring good luck for the year ahead.

Details from sleeve band decoration

A lovely butterfly attracted to fragrant garden flowers

The chrysanthemum was carefully cultivated in China

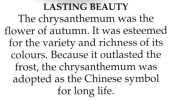

The peach is a symbol of eternal life

Arts and crafts

C HINA HAS ALWAYS BEEN RENOWNED for its exquisite arts and crafts. In imperial China, luxury goods formed the major export commoditie – Chinese bronze, jade, silk, lacquer, and porcelain were prized in Asi and Europe. Although the manufacture of decorative objects involved sophisticated techniques, many were mass-produced. From the Shang dynasty onwards, Chinese rulers controlled the supply of raw materials and ran government factories. These wer manned by skilled artisans who carried out the different stages of the manufacturing processe Unlike the merchants who sold their handiwork, artisans were well thought of i China. After the scholars and the peasant farmers, artisans were considered the mos important members of society. They produced tools for agriculture and weapon for the army as well as luxury items such as decorated tableware and fine silk cloth.

BEAUTIFUL BRONZE
In ancient China, bronze was made into stunning ritual vessels and weaponry. This circular fitting, which dates from Shang times, probably decorated a harness or a shield. Later, in about the 6th century B.C., the Chinese refined the process of iron casting. From then on government iron foundries produced iron and even steel in bulk.

Lead glazes run to give a swirly pattern

Underside of teacup

Mother-of-pearl inlay

POTS OF STYLE
China is famous for its beautiful, high-quality ceramics. This is due partly to the rich deposits of suitable clay and porcelain stone found in China. Over the centuries Chinese craftsmen developed a wide range of innovative techniques for making and decorating ceramics. One of the most famous styles was the "blue and white" porcelain manufactured in the Ming dynasty. Large amounts of this were exported to Europe from the 15th century onwards. Another distinctive style was the "three-colour" pottery popular in the Tang dynasty. This was decorated with three colours of lead glaze to create bold, splashy patterns, as seen on the Tang teacups above.

FIT FOR A KING
This exquisite box from the Ming dynasty is made from lacquered basketry inlaid with mother-of-pearl. It is decorated with a romantic scene showing a scholar taking leave of his friends. A lacquered finish took many days to produce and was usually highly decorated. Since lacquer ware was both expensive and beautiful, it was often given as an imperial gift to neighbouring rulers. In Korea and Japan Chinese lacquer was greatly admired.

BURNISHED GOLD
Some of China's finest pieces of art were religious or ceremonial objects. This beautiful gilt bronze figure represents the Buddha of Immeasurable Light. Chinese craftsmen often decorated the Buddha with bright, shining gold, or gilt, to emphasize his holiness.

Gold leaf or gold dust is applied to bronze to give a bright finish

Bronze Buddha, Ming dynasty

RAINBOW COLOURS
This lovely Qing-dynasty fish vase is decorated with cloisonné enamel. This enamelling technique was a foreign invention first produced in China in the early Ming dynasty. At first, many Chinese thought the bright colours used for cloisonné ware were vulgar, but by the 15th century cloisonné was used to decorate spectacular palace ornaments.

E MOST PRECIOUS STONE
e was highly prized by the nese from ancient times. s lustrous gemstone rs in soft greens, ys, and browns, d is satiny smooth en polished. e Chinese ieved that e was vested h magical perties, and as long been ociated with mortality.

The fish is a sacred Buddhist symbol that presents spiritual liberation

A vase symbolizes immortality

Enamel paste is applied to tiny metal compartments called cloisons

Treating silk cocoons

Gilt finish

LOWER MADE FROM A HORN
jects carved from rhinoceros horn re collectors' items in imperial ina. From the Tang dynasty, noceros-horn cups were presented special gifts to scholars who were ccessful in their civil service minations. The Daoists believed t rhinoceros-horn objects possessed gical powers. The rhinoceros-horn above is carved in the shape of a us blossom, a sacred Daoist flower.

SILK PRODUCTION LINE
The Chinese made silk from at least 3,000 B.C. In imperial China, silk manufacture was a well-organized state industry. Artisans produced large quantities of fine silk cloth in a myriad of rich colours. This luxury fabric was worn by scholars, civil servants, and emperors, and was exported to Asia and Europe along the Silk Road.

Ceremonial conch with silk tassel

The Silk Road

TRADE FLOURISHED under the Mongol, or Yuan dynasty. The Mongol emperors ruled China from 1279 to 1368 and permitted merchants to trade freely throughout their vast empire. They controlled the entire length of the Silk Road, a series of trade routes that ran from northern China across Asia. International trade thrived because caravans could travel without danger. Chinese merchants amassed large fortunes by exporting luxury goods such as silk, spices, teas, porcelain, and lacquer ware. At home in China, the Mongols removed the usual restraints placed upon merchants. Traditionally, merchants were excluded from civil service jobs and were subject to heavy taxes. But for most of their rule, the Mongols ignored the opinions of Chinese officials and the social position of merchants temporarily improved.

THE MONGOL CONQUEST
The Mongols came from north of the Great Wall. They were herdsmen who had expert cavalry skills, which made their army virtually unbeatable. After years of fighting, Genghiz Khan (1167–1227) conquered China. By 1279, the empire was under complete Mongol control. Genghiz Khan's grandson, Kubilai Khan, ruled almost the whole of East Asia until his death in 1294.

PORCELAIN PERFECTION
This magnificent porcelain jar from the Yuan dynasty is an example of the finely crafted ceramics that were exported to Asia and Europe. The "blue and white" style became widely popular in the Ming dynasty, which succeeded the Yuan.

"Blue and white" jar, 14th century

THE LAND OF SILK
The Silk Road took its name from China's most successful export commodity – silk. From the early empire onward the Chinese exported fine silk cloth to Asia and Europe. The Romans knew China as Serica, which means "Land of Silk". The secret of silk making was eventually smuggled out of China, but the Chinese remained the major exporters of silk to Europe until the 19th century.

Butterfly

Peony

Knife-shaped bronze coin, c. 500 B.C.

Hole allowed coin to be threaded on a string

A standard round coin introduced by the First Emperor

Silver pieces, used as money throughout the Chinese empire

Money shaped like a shoe

MAKING MONEY
In ancient times, travelling merchants used silver money shaped like knives or spades. The First Emperor introduced round bronze coins, known as *cash*. They remained in use for over 2,000 years. Paper money first appeared in the 11th century and was widely used in the Yuan dynasty.

Clipped coin

Silver ingot

Standard-size bolts of silk cloth were used as money between the Han and Tang dynasty

During the Yuan dynasty the Khans kept the peace along the Silk Road, which allowed foreigners to make the treacherous journey from Europe to China. Marco Polo (1254–1324) was a Venetian merchant who travelled to China, then known in Europe as Cathay, in the 13th century. He became a favourite of Kubilai Khan and served as an esteemed official in his civil service for nearly 20 years. After his return to Italy, Marco Polo wrote his famous *Travels*. This book gave Europe its first glimpse of the fabulous wealth and culture of the Chinese empire.

mels formed long
ravans that
velled along
e Silk Road

Saddle

Water bottle

Kubilai Khan with
his horsemen

THE LONGEST JOURNEY
The Silk Road wound its way
across the dry, barren lands that
linked the oasis-cities of central
Asia. Camels were the only beasts
of burden that could survive these
harsh conditions. They carried
only luxury goods because
transport was expensive
and difficult.

IE GREAT KHAN
bilai Khan's reign (1216–94) in China
as at the highest point of Mongol power.
e Mongol empire stretched from Asia
Europe, although expeditions sent
conquer Japan and Java failed.
bilai Khan established a
ttering capital at Kanbula,
hich is present-day
ijing. However, after the
eat Khan died, the
ongol emperors
uggled to maintain
ntrol over China. In
68, the Chinese Ming
nasty succeeded in
iving the Mongols
ck into Mongolia.

Ceramic Bactrian
camel, Tang dynasty

Great ocean voyages

AFTER THE MONGOLS WERE DRIVEN out of China, the emperors of the Ming dynasty (1368–1644) felt they needed to restore Chinese prestige. They strengthened the Great Wall, improved the Grand Canal, built a new capital at Beijing, and dispatched Admiral Zheng He to visit foreign rulers. Between 1405 and 1433, Zheng He led seven expeditions into the "Western Ocean". As a result, more foreign rulers than ever before recognized the ascendancy of the Chinese empire. Even distant Egypt sent back an ambassador to Beijing. Unlike European ships, which soon arrived in this part of the world, Zheng He's great fleet was not used to set up forts, control trade, or capture slaves. His voyages were peaceful demonstrations of Chinese naval power. When an African king sent a giraffe as a gift, Emperor Yong Le thought it was "a sign of perfect virtue, perfect government, and perfect harmony in the empire and the world".

A FLEET OF JUN
At the time of Admiral Zheng H voyages, no fleet in the world co match the great ships of the Chin navy. Zheng He commanded a fl of ocean-going junks, the traditio kind of Chinese sailing vessel. So of these junks are known to have h a displacement of 1,500 tonnes. Th were five times the size of Vasco Gama's ships, which rounded Cape of Good Hope and sailed i the Indian Ocean 70 years lat

The stiffened lugsail was a Chinese invention

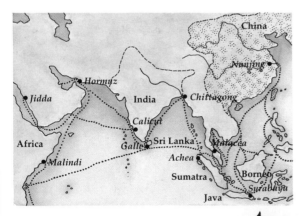

ZHENG HE'S VOYAGES
The map above shows the routes taken by Zheng He. In 1405 he was dispatched on his first expedition by the Ming emperor Yong Le (1402–24). On this voyage Zheng He visited Java, Sumatra, Malacca, Sri Lanka, and India. He took a great fleet of 317 ships manned by 27,870 men. Later, Zheng He visited Arabia and the east coast of Africa.

Painted eye for the boat to see with

A 20th-century illustration of Admiral Zheng He

閩 3179

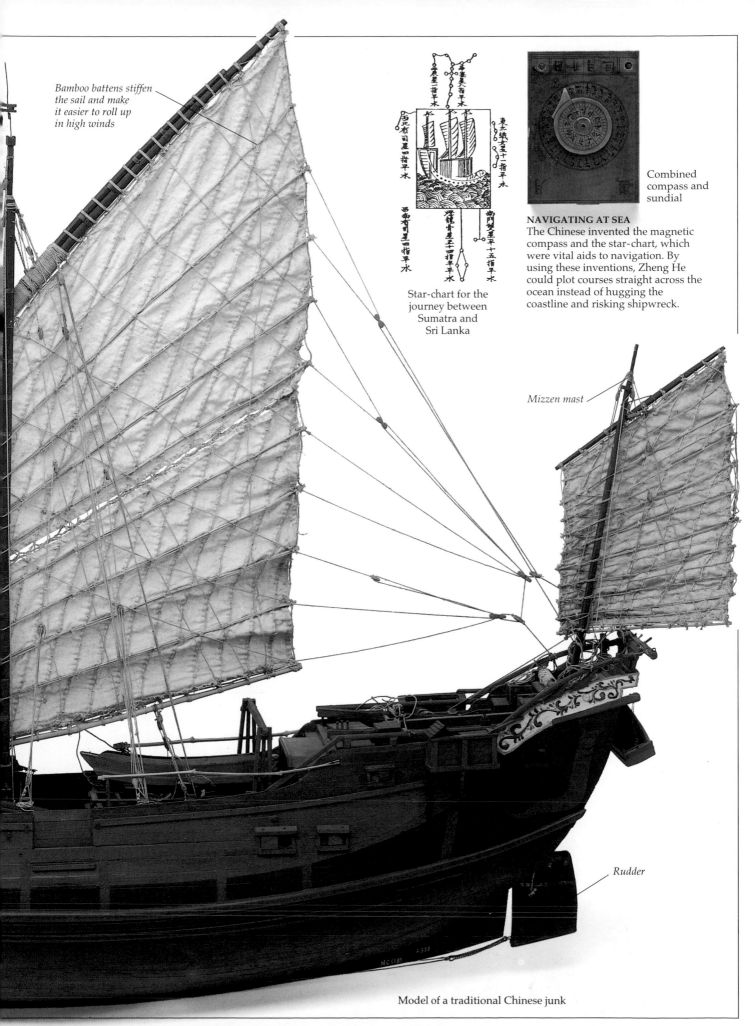

Bamboo battens stiffen the sail and make it easier to roll up in high winds

Star-chart for the journey between Sumatra and Sri Lanka

Combined compass and sundial

NAVIGATING AT SEA
The Chinese invented the magnetic compass and the star-chart, which were vital aids to navigation. By using these inventions, Zheng He could plot courses straight across the ocean instead of hugging the coastline and risking shipwreck.

Mizzen mast

Rudder

Model of a traditional Chinese junk

The end of the empire

DURING THE LAST 250 YEARS of the Chinese empire, the throne was occupied by the Manchus, a non-Chinese people from north of the Great Wall. China prospered for the first 150 years of the Manchu, or Qing dynasty (1644–1911). The emperors Kangxi (1662–1722) and Qianlong (1736–95) were enlightened rulers who supported Chinese art and culture and maintained the imperial civil service. However, the Qing emperors feared that change might lead to a Chinese rebellion and they clung to outdated traditions. For the first time, Chinese technology fell behind other countries. Britain, France, Russia, and later Japan began to bully the vulnerable Qing empire in order to gain trade concessions. In 1839 a Chinese official in Canton tried to stop the import of opium, which British ships brought from India to exchange for tea. After a clash, Britain declared war upon China and secured a swift victory. This encouraged other countries to demand trade concessions and awards of territory. The Qing dynasty failed to keep foreign powers at bay, and in 1900 an international force captured Beijing. In 1911, the Chinese overthrew their weakened Manchu rulers and set up a republic. The last Qing emperor, the infant Puyi (1906–67), was forced to step down in 1912, bringing to an end 2,000 years of imperial history.

A WISE RULER
The second Qing emperor, Kangxi, successfully secured Manchu rule in China. He was a wise emperor who respected Chinese culture. Unlike the previous foreign rulers, the Mongols, Kangxi employed Chinese scholars in the civil service. Many Chinese became loyal to the Qing dynasty.

PATRON OF THE ARTS
Kangxi's grandson Qianlong enjoyed a long and prosperous reign. He greatly admired Chinese art, which flourished under his patronage. Qianlong filled the imperial palace with a magnificent collection of paintings and artefacts, such as this beautiful elephant.

UNDER A FOREIGN HO
This painting shows the splendour of the Qing c
at Beijing. The Manchu, or Qing emperors admired
copied the sophisticated culture they had conquered,
they kept the Chinese firmly under control. Altho
Chinese scholars were recruited to the civil service, 50
cent of all appointments were reserved for Manchus.
emperor Qianlong feared that foreign ideas might ca
unrest among his Chinese subjects. For this reason
refused to allow more international tr

er rebels

BOXER REBELLION
900, the Boxers, an
-foreign society in
hern China, destroyed
orted goods and
cked Christian
sions. An international
e suppressed the uprising
occupied Beijing. It was the
straw for the Chinese empire.

BY FAIR MEANS OR FOUL
s priceless sceptre was presented to
e emperor Qianlong by the French.
the final years of the empire, there
s intense rivalry between European
powers to become the dominant
uence in China. France later seized
etnam, Laos, and Cambodia, which
were ancient Chinese allies.

OPIUM WAR
39, commissioner Li Zexu tried to
the British trading opium at the
of Canton. Britain sent gunboats to
ort the opium traders, and easily
ted the Chinese, as seen above.
British forced China to open four
ports to foreign trade and to
Hong Kong to Britain. This was
eginning of the end. Soon China
o open 10 more ports and
money and territory to foreign
rs such as France and Russia.

DEADLY TRADE
Opium was a drug used in China, but the
Qing emperors banned its import when
the British began to sell it in vast
quantities. The British traded
specially grown Indian
opium for tea and other
prized Chinese exports
because the Chinese
were uninterested in
British goods.

*The top of the
sceptre is made
in the shape of
a sacred
fungus*

*Sceptre
studded with
precious jewels*

19th-century
opium pipe

Qing good wishes
symbols

THE LAST EMPEROR
The last Qing emperor Puyi
(1909–1912) was placed on the
throne at the age of three. Only
three years later, revolutionaries
established a republican
government and forced him to
abdicate. Puyi was allowed to
remain in the Forbidden City
with his attendants, but
conditions worsened until he
fled to a Japanese colony in
1924. When the Japanese
invaded Manchuria in 1931,
Puyi was made emperor of
their puppet state, renamed
Manzhouguo. After the war,
Puyi was imprisoned in China.
Freed in 1959, he spent his last
years in Beijing.

Did you know?

AMAZING FACTS

Chinese acrobats have performed dazzling feats of skill and daring for more than 2,500 years. Tightrope walking, juggling with both hands and feet, human pagodas, and conjuring acts have been traced back as far as the Han dynasty. The earliest acrobats used everyday objects such as tables, chairs, jars, plates, and bowls in their routines.

Dogs resembling the wrinkly Chinese Shar-Pei dog have been found in ancient paintings and statues dating back to the Han dynasty. These dogs were a common fixture on Chinese farms for hundreds of years, serving as guard dogs and herders. Their natural scowling expression was thought to deter bandits and thieves, and their distinctive blue-black tongue was believed to ward off evil spirits.

Shar-Pei

Chinese people have been using chopsticks to eat food for about 5,000 years. Historians think that as the Chinese population grew, people had to conserve cooking fuel by chopping food into small pieces before cooking it, so that it cooked quickly. These bite-sized foods eliminated the need for knives at the dinner table. Chopsticks are usually made from bamboo, although they may also be made from other woods, plastic, porcelain, animal bone, ivory, coral, jade, or metal. Emperors and aristocrats preferred to use silver chopsticks, since they thought that silver would change colour if it came into contact with any poison.

The earliest examples of Chinese writing are the inscriptions on the oracle bones made in the late Shang period (c. 1200 B.C.). These artefacts were discovered by accident. In 1899, a Beijing man suffering from an illness was prescribed a remedy containing "dragon bones," or animal fossils, widely used in Chinese medicine. He noticed some carved patterns on the bones that looked like writing. Scholars later concluded that these carvings were written records dating back about 3,000 years.

Chopsticks

Chinese astrology has been practised since 550 B.C. According to Chinese legend, the order of the 12 astrological signs was determined by Buddha. The Buddha invited all the animals in the kingdom to gather for a meeting, but only 12 arrived: rat, ox, tiger, cat, dragon, snake, horse, goat, monkey, rooster, dog, and pig. To honour them, Buddha gave each animal a year of its own, bestowing the nature and characteristics of each animal to people born in that animal's year.

Monkey

During the Han dynasty, people in the upper classes seemed to put everything they might possibly need in the afterlife in their tombs. A few of a dead person's actual belongings were buried in the tomb, and miniature clay models were made of everything else. Typical models included horses and other farm animals, grain silos, servants, household goods, as well as small models of their above-ground homes.

Tomb animal

There was a flourishing of the arts in the Tang dynasty. Huge orchestras with as many as 700 instruments performed at the Imperial Court. Some people preferred "bird concerts". Bird lovers typically gathered together once a week in the mornings, bringing their caged friends with them to "sing" for the assembled crowds.

According to ancient Chinese legends, silk was discovered in 3,000 B.C. by Lady Xi Ling Shi, wife of the Emperor Huang Di. A silkworm cocoon accidentally dropped into her hot tea. Fine threads from the cocoon unravelled in the hot water, and silk was discovered. The Chinese fiercely guarded the secrets of silk-making; anyone who smuggled silk worm eggs or cocoons outside China was punished by death.

The Chinese lantern is an important symbol of long life and a supreme totem of good luck. Originating as far back as 250 B.C., the basic lantern has not changed. The sleeve or frame that surrounds the candle is assembled from bamboo or redwood. Thin or oiled paper, gauze, or silk, in the sacred shade of vermillion red covers the frame. The rounded shape is considered lucky because it resembles money. Lanterns were once symbols of a family's wealth. The richest families had lanterns so large, it required several people with poles to hoist them into place.

In ancient China, simple firecrackers were made by roasting bamboo to produce a loud cracking sound (similar to popping corn). This noise was thought to frighten away evil spirits. The discovery of gunpowder brought much more bang to Chinese fireworks, which became an important part of any celebration.

In the Tang dynasty, anyone with an education was expected to greet as well as say goodbye to another person in poetic verse, composed on the spot. In fact, every social occasion called for a poem, and poetry contests were very popular. Occasionally a few poets achieved national fame by having verses they composed transformed into popular songs by courtesans and entertainers.

Giant pandas date back two to three million years. The early Chinese emperors kept pandas because they were believed to ward off evil spirits, as well as natural disasters. They were also considered a symbol of might and bravery.

Pandas live almost entirely on bamboo

Giant panda

QUESTIONS AND ANSWERS

Q What is the history of the Great Wall of China?

A In ancient times, there were many smaller walls protecting China. During the 3rd century B.C., a unified wall was built to deter raiding tribes from modern-day Mongolia and Manchuria. Workers were pulled in from all over China; many of them died during the construction period. The present-day wall was built near the same site, mainly during the Ming dynasty (1368–1644). The Great Wall winds along the southern edge of the Mongolian plain, across deserts, grasslands, mountains, and plateaus, for an astonishing 2,414 km (1,500 miles). Built entirely by hand, it averages 7.6 m (25 feet) high and is 4.6–9.1 m (15–30 ft) thick at its base, tapering to a thinner top. Since 1949, two sections of the wall near Beijing have been reconstructed and are currently open to visitors.

The Great Wall of China

Q When were the terracotta warriors and horses discovered?

A In 1974, a group of farmers digging for a well in the Shaanxi province uncovered some bits of very old pottery. This drew the immediate attention of archaeologists, because the pottery fragments were so close to the unexcavated tomb of the First Emperor. Once experts had established that these artefacts were associated with the Qin dynasty, they arrived in droves. What they found became one of the most astonishing archaeological excavations of the 20th century. The tomb itself, rumoured to contain rare gems and other treasures, has still not been excavated.

The terracotta warriors

Q When and why was the Grand Canal constructed?

A The Grand Canal, the world's oldest and longest canal, is 1,795 km (1,114 miles) long, with 24 locks and around 60 bridges. The canal was built as a commercial waterway to connect the "rice bowl" agricultural regions in the south with the dry northern plains. The oldest section, linking the Yangtze and Huang He rivers, was built in the 4th and 5th centuries B.C. By the mid-19th century, the canal had fallen into disrepair, but the government dredged, repaired, and modernized the system in the early 1960s. Today, tourists can take boat trips up and down the canal.

Boats on the Grand Canal

Q What is China's Forbidden City and who lived there?

A The Imperial Palace in the heart of Beijing was the residence of emperors for nearly 500 years. Popularly known as the Forbidden City, it was built in the Ming dynasty between 1406 and 1420. This palatial complex is surrounded by 3-m (10-ft) high walls, and a deep moat. Its buildings represent the largest and best-preserved examples of Chinese traditional architecture in existence. The Outer Court was the seat of government and the site of important ceremonies, while the Inner Court was the residential area for the emperor and the imperial household.

Q What is the Summer Palace? Who created it, and why?

A Located just northwest of Beijing, the Summer Palace, built as a gift for the emperor's mother, is the largest imperial garden in the world and an incredible example of classical Chinese gardening and architecture. Construction began in 1750 and took 15 years to complete. The park is a vast landscape of hills and water, dotted with temples. Tourists can now enjoy what was once the private retreat of the imperial family.

Q What is the Shaolin Temple? Why is it important?

A Probably the most famous temple in China, the Shaolin Temple is renowned for its role in the development of both Chinese Buddhism and the martial arts. The temple was established in 495 in the Songshan Mountains to house Batuo, a celebrated Indian monk. In 537, another monk, Bodhidharma, settled in the temple. Legend has it that after meditating in a cave for nine years, he created a form of primitive boxing that became known as kung fu. After a tiny army of Shaolin monks scored an impressive defeat using kung fu, the temple became a thriving centre for Chinese kung fu masters.

Record Breakers

TOTAL NUMBER OF EMPERORS IN ANCIENT CHINA
There were 157 emperors, over a period of more than 2,000 years.

FIRST EMPEROR
Ying Zheng, who gave himself the title Qin Shi Huangdi, was the first to rule all of China.

OLDEST EMPEROR
Emperor Wu Di died at age 70, after ruling for an incredible 54 years.

ONLY EMPRESS
Empress Wu Zetian ruled from 690 to 705.

LONGEST REIGN
Kangxi ruled from 1661 to 1772.

SHORTEST REIGN
Taichang ruled for only one month, in 1620.

Timeline

THE CHINESE PEOPLE HAVE SHARED A COMMON culture longer than any other group of people. Dynasties were launched and overturned, emperors rose to power or were crushed in defeat, but the basic system of rule established in 221 B.C. survived until 1912. In addition, the Chinese people have maintained their cultural identity throughout their tumultuous history by means of a stable social structure and a 4,000-year-old writing system. Here is a timeline to key events.

Neolithic Chinese jar

Animal-face handles, Han dynasty

C. 10,000 B.C.

The Early Neolithic period begins in China. As in other parts of the world, Neolithic settlements grow up along the main river systems. In China, the dominant rivers are the Yellow River in central and northern China, and the Yangtze in southern and eastern China.

C. 5000 B.C.

Farming villages are established along the Yellow River valleys. People use polished stone tools, keep pigs and dogs, and grow millet, wheat, and barley. They make pottery jars to store their food, which are formed by stacking coils of clay into the desired shape and smoothing the surfaces with paddles. The pottery is decorated with red and black pigments, and features images of plants, animals, and humans. Each village is made up of a cluster of houses around a large central building for meetings, and has a public cemetery behind the houses.

C. 4500 B.C.

Early rice farmers build houses on stilts near the Yangtze River. Their pottery differs in shape from that of their northern neighbours, and includes tripod-shaped pottery. They later develop a potter's wheel. They make beautiful carvings on stone, bones, and jade – a very difficult and time-consuming substance to work with due to its hardness.

C. 3000 B.C.

The Bronze Age begins in China. In contrast to the European Bronze Age, the Chinese do not make bronze farming tools. Instead, they make elaborate bronze items for use in religious ceremonies.

Jade tortoise

Silk tomb draping

C. 1650–1027 B.C.

The Shang dynasty establishes its rule in the central plains. The Shang build walled towns and cities, palaces, royal tombs, and workshops for making bronze objects. Many Shang bronzes feature a distinctive two-eyed mask design called the taotie (monster face). Shang artisans also carve in jade. The first Chinese writing probably emerges during this time.

1027–256 B.C.

The Zhou dynasty begins after the Shang are defeated in battle. The Zhou king divides up the land into huge estates. He gives control of these estates, as well as chariots, textiles, and slaves, to his relatives. These lords rule over the peasants and slaves, who work the land. The Zhou reign longer that any other dynasty.

481–221 B.C.

The Warring States period begins as the kings and lords of the Zhou begin to lose control of the country. The lords turn on each other in an attempt to gain land, staging enormous battles in which hundreds of thousands of warriors lose their lives. Early Chinese scholars react to this situation by creating new ways of thinking about the world, which we now call philosophy.

C. 400 B.C.

The earliest exising paintings on silk date to this time.

551 B.C.

Chinese philosopher Confucius is born. During his lifetime, he has many rivals, but his teachings later become the basis for the state religion of China and are followed by every Chinese official.

Statue of Confucius

221–207 B.C.

The Qin dynasty (pronounced "chin," therefore providing the Western name for China) begins, when the Qin state in the northwest of China unites the whole country. The king of Qin becomes the First Emperor of China. He builds lavish palaces and erects stone tablets praising his achievements. To strengthen his rule, he orders that all works of literature and philosophy be burned, and 500 scholars are buried alive. Under this dynasty, the Chinese script, currency, and system of measurements are standardized. The emperor also creates the Great Wall of China (in part from existing walls) to protect his empire, and an army of terracotta soldiers to protect him in the afterlife.

207 B.C.–A.D. 220

The Han dynasty begins after a peasant uprising overthrows the Qin dynasty shortly after the death of the First Emperor. The Han establish a civil service that helps to govern China's population for the next 2,000 years. The western Han capital, Chang'an, is a huge urban centre with palaces, government buildings, houses, and markets, and is one of the two largest cities in the ancient world (the other being Rome). Agriculture and industry develop rapidly during this period, and ox ploughs and iron tools are in widespread use. Poetry, literature, and philosophy flourish.

138 B.C.

Emperor Wu Di sends an official named Zhang Qian on a second trip to central Asia to seek allies (on an earlier trip, Qian had been captured and held hostage by Huns). Qian is the first person to record anything about central Asia and its people, and trade between central Asia and China along the Silk Road increases.

C. A.D 100
The earliest-known example of hemp paper with Chinese writing on it dates to around this time.

A.D 221–589
Period of disunity as the Han dynasty is under pressure from rebels. People rise up against the Han dynasty, eventually bringing about its collapse. During this troubled time, the faith known as Buddhism takes hold in China. Paper, probably invented in the second century B.C., comes into widespread use as methods of paper-making improve.

A.D 589–618
The Sui dynasty reunites northern and southern China, and a period of prosperity and growing influence in the world begins. The Great Wall of China is repaired and expanded, and the Grand Canal linking the Yangtze and Yellow rivers is dug. The opening of this waterway strengthens trade and communication links around the empire.

A.D 618–907
The Tang dynasty rules during what is known as the Golden Age of Chinese history. In the early years of the Tang, nomadic tribes in the north are subdued, bringing peace and safety along the trade routes. Men with merit (but without family connections) are finally allowed to join the government. The population grows and both agriculture and textile production increase. Chinese art and literature flourishes during this dynasty, as exemplified by the poets Li Bai and Du Fu, the painter Wu Daozi, and the poet/painter Wang Wei.

C. A.D 700
The Tang capital city of Chang'an is now the world's largest and richest city. It is surrounded by a wall with 12 ornate gateways, and contains a huge palace and garden. Merchants from all over the world flock to the city to buy and sell goods. An early banking system is established to make business transactions easier.

C. A.D. 750
Drinking tea as a leisure activity becomes popular. In earlier times, tea was used chiefly as a medicine.

C. A.D. 868
The technique of woodblock printing is perfected. The earliest-known printed book, a Buddhist text called the *Diamond Sutra*, is made in China using woodblock printing.

A.D 907–960
The Five Dynasties period begins when a peasant rebellion brings down the Tang dynasty. China is divided into north and south. A number of short-lived kingdoms spring up in the north, while the south is divided into small states.

A.D 960–1279
The Song dynasty emerges to reunite China in an era of great social and economic change. Metalwork, lacquer, textiles, and other luxury goods are produced for domestic use and trade. Fine porcelain and green-glazed celadon wares are particularly important traded goods. Printing and paper-making also develop quickly, and artists paint enormous landscapes. Paper money is also invented during this era.

c. 1020
The Song government encourages the spread of schools and provides support for them across China.

c. 1041
Bi Sheng invents movable type for printing. He makes a separate block for each character out of clay. The blocks can be arranged for printing and then reused.

c. 1044
The earliest formula for making gunpowder is recorded.

c. 1050
Printed books are in widespread use across China. Books and paper are also exported to other lands along trade routes.

c. 1088
Han Gonglian designs the first water-driven astronomical clock. It takes three years to construct this elaborate device, complete with 200 wooden puppets that beat drums.

Paper-making mould

Diamond Sutra scroll

c. 1200
Genghiz Khan unites several nomadic tribes to establish the Mongol empire.

c. 1271
Marco Polo, the son of a merchant from Venice, Italy, arrives in China. He remains there for more than 20 years. On his return, he dazzles Europeans with reports of what he has seen.

1279–1368
The Yuan dynasty established after Kubilai Khan (Genghiz Khan's grandson) leads the Mongolian army into battle against the Song dynasty and wins. The Mongols, now in control of the entire Silk Road, focus on international trading. Many Europeans begin to make their way to China, taking Chinese innovations and inventions back to the West.

1368–1644
The Ming dynasty begins as the Chinese push out the Mongols. This is the last Chinese dynasty. Ming emperors build most of what we now see of the Great Wall, and improve the Grand Canal. The Ming dynasty is famous for its beautiful arts and crafts, especially blue and white ceramic wares.

Ming vase

1405–1433
Chinese explorer Zheng He makes his seven voyages of discovery. His travels take him to Southeast Asia, India, the Persian Gulf, and East Africa. His fleet is the largest in the world at the time.

c. 1406
Construction begins on the Forbidden City, which will remain home to China's emperors until the end of the imperial era.

1644–1912
The Qing dynasty (led by the Manchu, a semi-nomadic people from northeast of the Great Wall) capture the Ming state. For the first time, Chinese technology lags behind the rest of the world, as the Qing cling to outdated traditions. Pressure from foreign countries to allow trading within China builds; after the Opium Wars (1839 and 1856) China is forced to concede both trading rights and territory.

1912
The Chinese republic is established and the last emperor, Puyi, steps down. He is allowed to remain in the Forbidden City until 1924.

Puyi, c. 1940

Find out more

IF YOU ARE EVER LUCKY ENOUGH TO JOURNEY TO CHINA, you will be able to visit some of the incredible places in this book and explore the rich history of imperial China. But you may not have to travel that far to find out more about Chinese history. Most large museums contain stunning examples of Chinese artefacts, from tools to textiles. A visit to your local Chinatown will give you a taste of Chinese culture, especially if you stop for a meal. You can also explore the cultural history of China by attending an arts event.

WOK AND ROLL
The art of cooking has been celebrated in China since ancient times. The once-exotic spices, herbs, and vegetables that have been found in Chinese kitchens for centuries are now easy to buy almost anywhere. Cooking up a delicious stir-fried meal in a Chinese wok is fun, fast, and healthy. Sign up for a Chinese cooking class, or look for tasty recipes in a cookery book or on the Internet.

DOWN TO CHINATOWN
If there is a city in your area with a Chinatown, a stroll through its streets can be a fun way to find out more about Chinese culture. Peer inside a traditional Chinese medicine shop, explore the busy open-air markets, and stop for a bite to eat. Plan your visit to coincide with one of the major Chinese festivals – Lunar New Year, the Autumn Moon Festival, the Winter Solstice Lantern Procession, and the Dragon Boat festival are celebrated with fairs, parades, storytelling, crafts, special foods, and fireworks.

Dragon dancers hoist a colourful silk dragon in a festival parade

SEE CHINESE ACROBATS
Chinese acrobatics has evolved into a leading art form over thousands of years. Attend a performance, and you will see why these performers were the favourites of emperors and commoners alike. It takes years of training and discipline for acrobats to reach this level of skill. You will be astounded by their daring and sheer precision. Check your newspaper entertainment listings or use the Internet to locate a performance.

USEFUL WEBSITES

www.ancientchina.co.uk/menu.html
The British Museum's guide to ancient China

www.historyforkids.org/learn/china/
A cool learning site for children dedicated to ancient and Medieval China, with plenty of activities

www.asianart.com
A guide to the art of ancient China and Asia

www.mnsu.edu/emuseum/prehistory/china
An easy-to-follow timeline and history of China

TRY AN ANCIENT CHINESE CRAFT

Anyone can put pen to paper, but imagine how interesting it would be if that pen were a Chinese calligraphy brush, and the paper made by hand! Contact your local arts centre (or ask the art teacher at school) if there are calligraphy or paper-making classes held near where you live, and try your hand at these ancient Chinese arts.

Students wear traditional clothing when they learn kung fu

TAKE KUNG FU LESSONS

For children, martial arts training has many rewards, from increased self-confidence and motivation to overall physical and mental health. It's also fun! Sign up to learn kung fu, and practice this ancient martial art developed thousands of years ago in China. A local community centre may be a good source for inexpensive classes, or you can check the Internet or telephone directory.

Chinese orchestra member plays a traditional instrument

SEE A CHINESE CONCERT

Listening to the traditional music of China is an ear-opening experience! The music of China is built on a different harmonic system than most Western music. This is a result of some of the amazing musical instruments used in Chinese music, from the *pipa* (grand lute) to the *erhu* (python-skin fiddle). Traditional Chinese orchestras often tour European cities, and many performance halls offer educational programmes to help listeners better understand the music.

Places to Visit

BRITISH MUSEUM, LONDON
This museum's comprehensive collection includes examples of Chinese calligraphy, ceramics, coins, jade carvings, lacquerware, paintings, sculptures, and textiles.

VICTORIA AND ALBERT MUSEUM (V&A), LONDON
The V&A's Far Eastern collection contains hundreds of objects from Ancient China, including ceramics, textiles, porcelain, snuff bottles, robes, and furnishings.

THE ASHMOLEAN MUSEUM OF ART AND ARCHAEOLOGY, OXFORD
One of the oldest public museums in the world, the museum includes many examples of Eastern art.

WORLD MUSEUM, LIVERPOOL
The museum's Asian collection tells the story of the trade in goods, ideas, and beliefs between Asian countries and Europe. Its collection includes ceramics, ivories, and furniture made in China for export.

ORIENTAL MUSEUM, UNIVERSITY OF DURHAM, DURHAM
This museum's China gallery includes a display of ceramics featuring earthenware storage jars from around 2,500 B.C., and porcelain tableware of the 18th, 19th, and 20th centuries. Its collection also includes objects made of bronze, ivory, and bamboo; examples of calligraphy; and paintings.

THE FAN MUSEUM, GREENWICH, LONDON
This small museum has over 3,500 fans on display and includes examples from all over the world.

SIR JOHN SOANES MUSEUM, LONDON
This small, packed museum contains over 300 Chinese tiles (said to be the most notable collection in the world) and a porcelain dinner service made for export with between 200-300 surviving pieces.

VISIT A MUSEUM'S CHINESE ART COLLECTION

One of the best ways to learn about the history of an ancient culture is through its art. From paintings to lacquerware, the beauty and depth of imperial Chinese art is amazing. Many museums, such as the Seattle Asian Art Museum (above), feature outstanding Chinese artefacts in their permanent collections.

Glossary

ACUPUNCTURE An ancient Chinese system of healing in which fine needles are inserted at specific points just under the skin to stimulate and disperse the body's flow of energy to relieve pain, or to treat a variety of different medical conditions.

Acupuncturist inserting needles

ANCESTOR Someone from whom a person is descended. The worship of ancestors has been important in China since the Neolithic age.

BODHISATTVA In Mahayana Buddhism, an enlightened being; a figure of profound compassion who has already attained enlightenment but postpones his or her own hope of reaching eternal peace by helping others who seek nirvana.

BRONZE An alloy of copper (usually about 90 per cent) and tin, often mixed with small amounts of other metals. Since ancient times it has been the metal most commonly used in casting sculptures, because it is strong, durable, and easy to work.

BUDDHA The founder of Buddhism, born in 563 B.C. as Siddhartha Gautama; a prince from northern India who devoted his life to seeking enlightenment, or personal peace.

BUDDHISM A major world religion based on the teachings of the Buddha. Buddhism took hold in ancient China and remains the country's most popular belief.

CALLIGRAPHY A style of beautiful handwriting created by using special pens and brushes.

CIVIL SERVICE A generic name for all the people employed by the government to carry out public services. Successful candidates need to pass tests called civil service examinations.

Calligraphy character

CIVILIZATION A culture; a particular society at a particular time and place.

CONFUCIANISM A philosophy based on the teachings of Confucius in the sixth century B.C. Followers of Confucianism hope to establish a better overall world by means of improving each individual within their society.

CONFUCIUS The ancient Chinese philosopher and sage who lived from 551 to 479 B.C. He became China's most influential philosopher and a leading political reformer.

Great cormorant

CORMORANT A dark-coloured Asian seabird that plunges into the water and snaps up fish. The cormorant stores its catch in a stretchy pouch of skin on its long neck.

CRIB Anything used to help a person cheat in an exam; for example, the handkerchief covered with civil-service-exam answers on page 19.

CROSSBOW A weapon for shooting arrows, consisting of a bow placed aross a wooden shaft that is grooved to direct an arrow.

DAOISM (or TAOISM) A system of philosophy that advocates a simple, honest life and cautions against interfering with the course of natural events.

DIVINATION STICKS Special sticks used to help people foretell the future, by connecting with divine spirits.

DYNASTY A succession of rulers from the same family or line; in imperial China, a succession of emperors who were related.

ELIXIR A mythical liquid thought to grant eternal life to anyone who drinks it; sought by both Chinese and European alchemists.

FERRULE A cap attached to the end of a shaft for strength or to prevent splitting.

FINIAL A decorative detail used to top an object. Manchu caps were topped with finials that showed a civil servant's rank.

GUNPOWDER A mixture of chemicals (usually potassium nitrate, charcoal, and sulphur) that was once used to ignite fireworks, or as a propellant charge. Also known as black powder.

HALBERD A shafted weapon with an axe-like cutting blade; similar to the Chinese quando.

INKSTONE A smooth, hard, shallow tray of stone or pottery, used in calligraphy to mix ink sticks or cakes with water.

IRON CASTING Using a steady blast of heat to produce a stronger form of iron; developed by the Chinese in the 6th century B.C.

JADE A semiprecious gemstone, usually green but sometimes whitish, that can be worked to a high polish.

JUNK A Chinese flat-bottomed sailing boat with a high stern.

LACQUER A waterproof varnish made by layering several coats of treated tree sap. Colours can be combined and layered in relief as well as carved. In Chinese art, the most popular colours are red and black. Lacquer is applied to wood, bamboo, cloth, ceramics, and metals.

LONG In Chinese mythology, the name for a type of majestic dragon that dwells in rivers, lakes, and oceans and also roams the skies. Long became the symbol of the Chinese emperor.

MAGNETIC COMPASS A handheld instrument with a magnet inside which pivots freely. Because Earth is a giant magnet, the magnet in the compass will always point toward the Earth's poles, to indicate north and south.

Divination stick

Bronze
halberd

MILLET A bland cereal grass that can be boiled for cereal or ground for flour.

MONGOL A member of the nomadic peoples of Mongolia, in Asia. In the 12th and 13th centuries, the Mongols conquered most of Asia and Eastern Europe and ran a vast trading empire.

MOTHER-OF-PEARL The hard, smooth, iridescent inner-shell lining of oysters, mussels, and other molluscs. Mother-of-pearl is milky white to silvery grey.

MOXIBUSTION Part of the traditional practice of acupuncture, involving burning the dried and crumbled leaves of an herb plant known as moxa near acupuncture points of the body.

NAIL GUARDS Decorative fingertip covers used to protect the long nails of the upper classes during the later years of the Chinese empire.

ORACLE BONES Animal bones or shells, inscribed with writing, used to foretell the future in ancient China. One famous set contains the oldest-known example of the Chinese written language.

Oracle bones

PADDY A field where rice is grown.

PAGODA An Eastern temple, particularly in the form of a multistorey, tapering tower, each storey having its own roof.

PEASANT A country person or small farmer.

PHILOSOPHY The study of, or search for, knowledge, wisdom, and an understanding of the nature of the universe.

PLOUGHSHARE In agriculture, a sharp steel wedge that cuts loose the top layer of the soil before planting.

PUFU A long Chinese coat worn over other clothing.

QIN Also known as Yang Qin, a stringed Chinese musical instrument resembling the Western zither.

REBELLION An organized opposition to authority.

SAMPAN A small Chinese boat, usually propelled by two oars.

SCROLL A roll of paper which is unfurled at one end and rolled up at the other to reveal its text.

SHENG A Chinese musical instrument similar to a harmonica, with 17 pipes extending upwards from a metal bowl.

SILK ROAD The historical trade route linking the Eastern Mediterranean basin with Central and East Asia. It got its name because of the silk, tea, and jade carried along the route from China.

SILKWORM A white caterpillar of the Chinese silkworm moth, which is the source of most commercial silk. Silkworms spin dense cocoons, each of which contains a single strand of interwoven silk.

TAOTIE A representation of a terrifying animal face with staring eyes, horns, and fangs, used on ritual objects in the Shang dynasty.

Taotie

TERRACOTTA A reddish brown clay that is fired but not glazed.

WOODBLOCK An ancient method of printing in which characters are carved in reverse on a wooden block. Inking the surface of the block and pressing it against a sheet of paper makes a print.

YIN AND YANG Two opposing forces in Chinese cosmology that together make up everything in the Universe. Yin is the feminine element, associated with night, and yang is the masculine element, associated with day.

Pagoda-style roof of the Daigo-ji Temple in Kyoto, Japan

Index

Acknowledgements

The publisher would like to thank:
The staff of the Department of Oriental Antiquities at the British Museum, London, in particular Chris Kirby, Jane Newson and Christine Wilson – with special thanks to Anne Farrer; the British Museum Photographic Department, especially Ivor Kerslake; Marina de Alarçon at the Pitt Rivers Museum, Oxford; Shelagh Vainker at the Ashmolean Museum, Oxford; John Osborne at the Museum of Mankind, London; Monica Mei at the Acumedic Centre, London; the Guanghwa Company Ltd., London; Helena Spiteri for editorial help; Sharon Spencer, Susan St. Louis and Isaac Zamora for design help.

Additional photography by Peter Anderson (62cl, 63cl), Matthew Chattle (50-51t), Andy Crawford (13tr), Philip Dowell (52cl), David Gowers (59c), Chas Howson (23cr, 58bl), Ivor Kerslake (40tl), Dave King

(2bl,cr, 40cl), Laurence Pordes (11cr, 19br, 24bl,cr, 25tl,bl), Ranald MacKecknie (54cl), and James Stevenson (23tl, 60-61c)
Maps by Simone End (6tl, 9br, 60bl)
Index by Hilary Bird

Picture credits
a=above, b=below, c=centre, l=left, r=right

Bridgeman Art Library/Bibliotheque Nationale, Paris 16cr, 27tl
By permission of the British Library 24cl
©British Museum 58cl,cr
J. Allan Cash Ltd. 6br
Courtesy Chinese Cultural Embassy 16cl
Comstock/George Gerster 16br, 35tl
Arthur Cotterell 15cl, 22c, 23tr, 24tc, 31tl, 32tr, 44tl,cl, 50br, 53cr, 55tl, 58tl, 62tl
R.V. Dunning FC tl,br, 18c,bc, 31tl, 41bc
ET Archive 34tl/Bibliotheque Nationale, Paris 18tl,39tl,54tl/British Museum FC bl, BC tc, 20tl, 38tl/Freer Gallery of Art 35cr,

36cr;/National Palace Museum, Taiwan 42bl;/Private Collection 62b;/Courtesy Trustees Victoria & Albert Museum 50cr, 57cr
Mary Evans Picture Library 8tr, 12tl, 59tr;/T'Ongjen Tschen Kierou King 28bl;/Petit Journal BC br, 63tl, Vittorio Pisari in La Tribuna Illustrata 63br
Robert Harding Picture Library 16tr;/Collection of the National Palace Museum,Taipei, Taiwan, Republic of China 59bl
Mansell Collection 26tr, 36tl
National Maritime Museum 63bl
The Needham Research Institute 16bl, 22br
The Nelson-Atkins Museum of Art, Kansas City, Missouri (Purchase: Nelson Trust) 33-1559, 33tr
Photographie Giraudon 40bl
Photostage/Donald Cooper 52tl
Roger-Viollet 60bl
©Science Museum 22bl
Courtesy Trustees of Victoria & Albert

Museum 46br, 54cl;/Ian Thomas BC tl, 16clb, 21t,bc, 54-5b, 63tr
Alamy: Panorama Stock Photos Co Ltd 65cl, 66tl; Helge Pedersen 68bl; Chuck Pefley 68cr
Corbis: 67br; Asian Art & Archaeology, Inc. 66bl; Dean Conger 65tr; Werner Forman 70br; Walter Hodges 69tl; Gunter Marx Photography 69bc; Royal Ontario Museum 66-67tc, 71br; Sakamoto Photo Research Laboratory 71bl
Getty Images: National Geographic 65bl
The Granger Collection, New York: 71br

Every effort has been made to trace the copyright holders. The publisher apologizes for any unintended omissions and would be pleased, in such cases, to add an acknowledgement in future editions.